Flourishing In Drought

A Sure Solution to Economic Crisis

Sola Alabi

Living Spring Publications Network
Living Spring Communications
P.O. Box 1961, Ogbomoso, Oyo State, Nigeria

Flourishing in Drought

Copyright @ 2017 by Sola Alabi

All rights reserved. No part of this publication may be reproduced, stored in a retrieval system, distributed, or transmitted in any form or by any means, including photocopying, recording, or other electronic or mechanical methods, without the prior written permission of the publisher or a license permitting restricted copying.

Publish by:
LIVING SPRING PUBLICATIONS NETWORK
Living Spring Communications
P.O. BOX 1961, Ogbomoso, Oyo State, Nigeria.
Tel: +2347030198431, +2348115213552
E-mail: livingspringpublication@gmail.com
www.livingspringpublication.org

ISBN: **9781977848529**
1977848524

Unless otherwise noted, all Bible quotations in this book are taken from the New King James Version. Copyright ©1982 by Thomas Nelson, Inc. Used by permission. All rights reserved.

Typesetting and Editing by:
Living Spring Publishing Team

DEDICATION
To all individuals, homes, firms and nations currently battling with drought-like challenges in the world.

CONTENTS

Acknowledgement
Forward
Preface
Chapter 1
What is a Drought?
Chapter 2
What Causes Drought
Chapter 3
Flourishing in Drought 1
Chapter 4
Flourishing in Drought 2
Chapter 5
From Bereavement and Captivity to Royalty
Chapter 6
From Adversity to Ruler-ship
Chapter 7
Bright in Storm
Chapter 8
Glowingin the Fire
Chapter 9
Prosperity during Famine
Chapter 10
Flourishing Despite Opposition
Epilogue
Appendix

ACKNOWLEDGEMENT

My soul magnifies the Lord, my spirit praise His name for giving me the privilege to be the vessel through which He released this kingdom mysteries to the world. This book is a divine response to the current global economic downturn and whatever drought-like challenges that anyone battles with. Jesus is the solution to all human perditions, challenges and problems.

Thank you dear Lord for calling me into partnership with you in the writing aspect of your kingdom business – I'm grateful. All glory, honour and praise of this work are to you. I loudly and unreservedly declared that this book is by you, in you and for you – the giver of all mysteries.

The moment the burden of writing this book came to me I know I will need the help of some virtuous, exposed and anointed professionals along the way. These men laboured not for show, but sacrificially. They sacrificed their time, comfort … to ensure that this work come out in the right form and at the right time.

Rev. DrG. E. Omodele read through the manuscript, offered valuable contribution and wrote the foreword. Dr Samson Olajide Olaniyan of Economics Department, Osun State University and Dn. Jesse Aremu, CEO, Jesses Professional Consult, Abujaalso perused the autograph, gave positive comments and wrote about the book.

Olukunle Ojo, our beloved brother came around while working on the book and offered to typeset some portion of it. Oluwatosin Oyebode did the textual and lexical editing despite his huge official responsibilities. I can't forget the timely encouraging words of Solomon Oladipupo and Remi Adejumo while this book was being written. The prayer and other supports of my beloved parents Mr and Dns S.A. Alabi is of high value, may you live to witness the fulfillment of several prophesies we had received from God in Christ's name.

Finally, my beloved wife Funke laboured along with me while writing the book. She organized conducive atmosphere for me, ensuring that I wasn't distracted during the many days of putting the received insights together. We shall together walk into the fullness of the fulfillment of God's mandate on our union in Jesus' name. Amen. To everyone who laboured on this kingdom work, I say, may God grant us more opportunity to pay the debt we owe our generation in Christ's name – we won't leave any debt unpaid.

FOREWORD

When experiencing hard times which may come to a person in different shape, form and size; irrespective of status, the natural response from majority of people whether religious or non-religious is to query God of why this happen to them. And immediately seek way out of it from other means other than looking unto God for solution. Among many, the most unpopular place to turn to for help in times of drought is trusting God for solution. In many cases not until when they have exploited all other means for solution and there seems to be no way that they often remember God.

In a time like this that nations and individuals are going through economic challenges and every known economic principles employed are failing and defying.All hope is not lost because where men scarcely looked for solution is where the potent secrets of flourishing in a time like this lies.

Thanks to God for the inspiration He has given to the author of this book to bring hope and assurance of flourishing when men's hearts are failing them. This book is all about hope for all that may be experiencing one form of drought or the other.According to the author, "It is written to enlighten people about the way out of spiritual, economic, material, professional, and social mess."

He has done a wonderful job of x-raying what drought is, the causes and interventions that people had experienced and resulted to their flourishing in the midst of drought. The exposition done in this book is a tremendous help that is coming at the most appropriate time. The book is very practical in its approach because the author exposes to us from the word of God how men and women and nations who turned to God were able to flourish in a time of drought.

I will like to recommend this book to all that are sincerely seeking the way out of their drought seasons. This book will let you see opportunities that abound all around you to explore in a time like this. It is also recommended to all who want to stay flourishing, that as you learn of what brings drought you will stay clear of them and continue to do the things that make you become a tree planted by the rivers of water that brings forth his fruit in season and do not know when drought comes.

In the final analysis, God still holds the key to the flourishing of our lives irrespective of what is happening worldwide. He is the Lord that calls things that are not as if they were and they came to be. *"You will keep him in perfect peace those whose minds are steadfast, because they trust in you. Trust in the LORD forever, for the LORD, the LORD Himself, is the Rock eternal." (Isaiah 26: 3-4)*

Rev Dr G. E. Omodele
Pastor, New Light Baptist Church, Magodo Phase II, Lagos, Nigeria.

PREFACE

There's not a friend like the lowly Jesus, No, not one! No, not one! None else could heal all our soul's diseases, No, not one! No, not one!
Jesus knows all about our struggles, He will guide till the day is done; There's not a friend like the lowly Jesus, No, not one! No, not one!

Johnson Oatman, Jr., 1856-1922

Many a times when we're faced with diverse challenges; persecutions, troubles and ridicule, we tend to consider or even conclude that God has forgotten us. Then, we ask series of questions like, "Why me? Why this time? Does God even see my troubles? Why did God permit this to happen to me? Does God even care at all?" And lots more.

We probe and interrogate God because to us God doesn't make sense during such a time. Meanwhile, it would have been fair on God if people had stopped at the juncture of, "God that's not fair!" But alas, when things really become so tensed, people doubt God's existence while some others went on cursing Him! The current global economic challenge(s) had disillusioned many – it had made some to misbehave while others had out-rightly abandoned their faith.

In it all you need to know that Jesus knows about your trouble. He sees your pains and agony. He is all knowing and all seeing – your pains are not hidden from Him. To say God doesn't see and know about your troubles and challenges is to doubt Him as God. He knows the state of your life, home, academics, profession, business, finance, health, nation…. The ups and downs in your life are obvious before Him. The ranging storm that buffets your marriage – your spouse and children that had grown wild – your lack or loss of job – the financial ridicule your home is experiencing are nothing hidden to Him.

The many years of admission challenge, lack of tuition fee, memory loss or brain block you're struggling with are all known to God. God sees how frustrated you are in your profession and business. He knows the federal government owes you some months' salary. He knows your state government has only been able to pay you half of your due salary.
He knows your household now scarcely eats the normal daily meal ration. He knows how jilted and frustrated you feel when your would-be spouse, brethren and loved ones disappointed you. He can see the confusions that have prevailed over the nations of the world. He knows the global economic meltdown had frozen your purse.

I'm glad to inform you that God knows our political leaders are even more confused than we the followers. He knows many of them don't even know what to do. It is clear to Him that many world leaders gamble at decisions; that's why virtually all the steps they had taken to solve the challenge of economic meltdown and others have yielded no positive result.

I am mandated to let you know that there is great light behind this season of thick dark cloud. I had to write this book at this time because there is a divine solution to the current challenge the world battles with. There is a solution to your life, family, spiritual, academic, professional, health, financial, psychological … challenges.

There is hope for our nation and the world. Our land can experience a turnaround if we would deal with God according to His terms. You, your nation and the world can flourish in this season of drought if you would follow the truths discussed in this book to detail.

This book defines what a drought is, what causes the experience of drought, how you and I and our nation can flourish during this season of global drought…. It also relays practical examples of people, cities and nations in history that applied the principles taught in this book and consequently flourished in their year of drought. This book is practical, emotional, compassionate, spiritual and straight forward. The use of simple grammar makes it helpful and applicable to all classes of men.

It speaks to individual, business executives, chief executive officers of companies, world leaders, kings, religious leaders and all other forms of rulers. My passion run through the pages of the book in these simple but compassionate expressions: "You can flourish in drought," "Your life, home and nation can experience a dramatic positive change not minding what had happen in the past," "Our nation can flourish in spite of the prevalent global economic meltdown," and lots more. I wish you experiential turn around as you read.

Sola Alabi
Living Spring Communications, Ede, Nigeria.
http://www.livingspringpublication.org

WHAT IS A DROUGHT?

Drought is Devastating, it's a Spiritual and Natural Reality!

Chapter 1
WHAT IS A DROUGHT?

Before going into practical issues, I need to define what a drought is. Drought connotes lack, deficiency, scarcity, dearth, shortage, famine, absence, want, starvation, deprivation, dispossession, deficit, inadequacies, paucity, infrequency etc. Drought is a situation of lack in the life, home, ministry, destiny, profession, economic, health … of a man.

It is a circumstance of deficiency in the performance, productivity, establishment, spiritual and physical growth and multiplication in a man's life. It's a condition of scarcity of grace, divine help, anointing, authority, mercy and favour. It defines a state of dearth when the heavens are negatively disposed toward a man, his home and endeavours.

Besides, it can also be defined as a context of shortage in growth, productivity, advancement, profit, success, fulfillment and income. It's an occurrence of famine where all 'trees' of production suddenly get dried, hence, stayed from productivity. It's a period of absence; absence of spiritual and physical rain and favour on a life, a people, group or society.

It's a time of want, starvation and deprivation when the minimum needs of people are not or cannot be met. Of course, in such a period, there will certainly be dispossession of goods and persons; as people will be ready to sell out their valuables for life sustenance. Deficits and inadequacies will be obvious in such a period – many people will go into debt. During drought, sicknesses, diseases, endemic plagues, and ultimately death are unavoidable.

Without doubt, the whole world is currently undergoing such a period. Many nations of the world are wallowing in situations that are exact or similar to the ones described above. We are in a period when government of nations could no longer cater for the constitutional needs of their citizens. Currently, there are nations in Africa, Europe and Asia that can't boast of having enough funds to run their annual budgets.

Economic recession had drastically affected the finance of nations as well as their growth, development and productivity. The situation had turned the wisdom of astute economists to foolishness – both their age long and modern day propounded principles had failed to salvage the downturn. The governments of some states are now running their agendas in deficit. When they can't financially sustain themselves, a number of nations currently look up to World Bank for loan.

When a nation government can't financially singlehandedly run her annual budget, what do you think would be the fate of her citizenry, dear reader? Citizens are doomed for starvation, want, inadequacies and debt. In Nigeria alone, about half of her state governments owe civil servants nothing less than six months' salary. When those in current service can't get their salary, what do you think will be the lot of retired staff? They are in for trouble, I think? That is the case! Most retired civil servants are denied of their gratuity and pension. Many of them have died of hunger, sicknesses and diseases – when they are denied of their due to take care of themselves.

The situation on ground had destabilized the order of things in the country. Instead of the citizens to be looking up to the government, the government currently looks up to people for finance. Some state governments had set up a number of means to exploit citizens. Various endemic plagues destroy people's life in interior villages, towns and cities.

The situation of drought in the world had promoted theft, harm robbery, prostitution, fraud, terrorism, human trafficking, militancy, kidnappings and corruptions of all kind. Currently, some corporate companies and industries have folded up, while others are embarking on staff retrenchment, due to the recession.

But in the midst of all these, is there hope of recovery? Is there anybody to help? Does anybody care for our restoration? Yes! There's hope. God made a provision for recovery from drought. He made a provision for recovery from the kind of mess the world has found itself. I mean there's hope for you, dear reader. No matter what may be the hardship, mess, ridicule or shame you currently experience, there's solution for you. Your life can bud, blossom and flourish again. You can yet sing a new song of victory in your life time.

You can recover all your lost fortunes. That's the purpose of writing this book. It's out to give hope to the hopeless. It's written to enlighten people about the way out of spiritual, economic, material, professional and social mess. Its purpose is to open people up to divine solution to drought-like experiences. If you'll carefully and staunchly believe and apply the truths presented here, your life, home, profession, church and community will experience dramatic change.

Before I proceed from here, I want you to read an infallible word of God that transfuses hope:

For there is hope for a tree, if it is cut down, that it will sprout again, and that its tender shoots will not cease.

Though its root may grow old in the earth, and its stump may die in the ground,

Yet at the scent of water it will bud and bring forth branches like a plant.
Job 14:7-9

After reading this book, may your life become a physical evidence to prove the efficacy of this scripture in Jesus' name. May your home and all that are yours become apparent audiovisual to prove the viability of the truth presented in the quoted text in Christ's name. Amen. Come along with me in this school of wisdom.

WHAT CAUSES DROUGHT

When the Cause of an Adversity is discovered its Solution is no Longer Far!

Chapter 2
WHAT CAUSES DROUGHT

Haven examined what drought is; now we would go into exploring series of things that causes drought. This chapter will help whoever is in drought to be able to trace what exactly led him or her into it. When he has discovered it, he can then go ahead to make necessary decision.

DISOBEDIENCE

This is the first major thing that causes drought for so many people on earth. Disobedience to God has ruined the lives and cut short the hope of countless men. Many previously blossoming children of God have entered into sudden but terrible obscurity because of disobedience. I think many don't know that God detests disobedience greatly and that's why the number of those who disobey Him on daily basis is on the high side.

"You have done foolishly. You have not kept the commandment of the Lord your God, which He commanded you. For now the Lord would have established your kingdom over Israel forever. But now your kingdom shall not continue" (1 Samuel 13:13-14) was God's response to the disobedient Saul. Disobedience can make God to reverse His promise over anyone. He's not a respecter of persons; once you disobey Him He dishes out your due punishment. As highly loving as God is, He hates disobedience.

You may wonder why God so uncompromisingly detests disobedience. You'll get clue to this now as you carefully read the text below:

> ***Has the Lord as great delight in burnt offerings and sacrifices, as in obeying the voice of the Lord? Behold, <u>to obey is better than sacrifice, and to heed than the fat of rams.</u>***
>
> ***<u>For rebellion is as the sin of witchcraft, and stubbornness is as iniquity and idolatry.</u> Because you have rejected the word of the Lord, He also has rejected you…*** 1 Samuel 15:22-23 (Emphasis mine)

Can you now see dear reader? God detests disobedience because obedience is better than sacrifice and to heed than the fat of rams. Also, He hates it because disobedience is the same as the sin of witchcraft and idolatry. Before God, disobedience has the same weight as the sin of witchcraft and idolatry. That's why He doesn't tolerate it.

Dear friend, have you begun to see from the above text how dangerous disobedience is? It leads men into drought. When God rejects a man, such a person automatically enters a season and situation of drought. God will shut the heavens over the person, and hence, all what he may have gathered in life will gradually crumble till he's left with nothing. Such an individual will begin to experience dryness in all areas of life. Do you doubt this? Meditatively read the Bible text below and your doubt will certainly disappear:

> *And after all this, if you do not obey Me, then I will punish you seven times more for your sins.*
>
> *I will break the pride of your power; I will make your heavens like iron and your earth like bronze.*
>
> *And your strength shall be spent in vain; for your land shall not yield its produce, nor shall the trees of the land yield their fruit.* Leviticus 26:18-20

That is God speaking out His mind. He said He'll punish whoever disobeys Him, He'll break the pride of his power, He'll make his heavens like iron and his earth or ground like bronze, and He'll cause the person to experience all-round lack of productivity. Is that not a drought? Certainly it is. Does this look like your experience, dear reader? Do you now suffer under terrible drought because of a disobedient act you committed in the past?

Is your wife and children now sharing in the awful consequences of your disobedience? Has your disobedience made God your enemy? Has He shut the heavens over your head to prevent grace, divine power, authority, and anointing ... from flowing to you? If that is your experience, you need to urgently cry to God in repentance before it'll be too late. He had promised:

> ***When I shut up heaven and there is no rain, or command the locusts to devour the land, or send pestilence among My people,***
>
> ***if My people who are called by My name will humble themselves, and pray and seek My face, and turn from their wicked ways, then I will hear from heaven, and will forgive their sin and heal their land.*** 2 Chronicles 7:13-14

Note dear friend that disobedience can be committed by an individual, a community, state or by a nation. But God's demand for restoration is still the same: Humble yourself, confess your sin(s)to Him in prayer and turn from your wicked ways. When you do this, He'll forgive you your sin(s) and heal your land by restoring your lost fortunes. Why will you delay? Take the step now to begin your process of restoration.

MISMANAGEMENT OF PUBLIC FUND

This has to do with those in government and various ministerial offices. A nation can be brought to a state of penury if those at the hems of affair love money than they love the people. Drought experience is certain for any nation whose leaders mismanage her fund and resources. Mismanagement of this kind can come in two major ways: fraud and misappropriation!

Dishonest use of money while in government will do no good for citizens; rather it'll bring hunger, want, disaster, and sometime untimely death in the future. To be honest, a great percentage of the economic challenges our nation is facing are caused by mismanagement of public fund. Many of our political leaders commit fraud and misappropriate.

The money meant for the masses are being shared by certain few people who were privileged to be in power. The Lord has to help us in this nation. Meanwhile, whoever is involved in this practice should repent lest God's wrath come on them, their spouse and children. Read what the Bible says:

*Like the partridge that gathers a brood which she did not hatch and sits on eggs which she has not laid, so is he who gets riches by unjust means and not by right. He will leave them, or they will leave him, in the midst of his days, and at his end he will be a fool.*Jeremiah 17:11 (AMP)

DRUNKENNESS AND ADULTERY

This is another agent of drought.We all know what drunkenness and adultery are. Drunkenness simply means having special crave and love for alcohol such that taking liquor daily has become an addiction. The drunkards don't stop taking alcohol daily till they have come to the level of intoxication.

Adultery on the other hand means extramarital activities. These two mentioned acts make whoever indulges in them to spend their income lavishly, such that they rarely have savings.

At least, I know a few persons who could have been wealthy in life by the virtue of their handwork, but wererendered paupers by drunkenness and adultery. I was oncea neighbour to a man who had prospect of riches, but lived and died poor because of his untamed love for alcohol and cigarette. While he was alive, he does not leave the beer pallor until he's totally drunk; he goeshome staggering.

The fact is, if you calculate the amount you daily spend on alcohol and adultery, then you'll know you are losing out a great deal of fortune. The money you, your wife and children would have used to live a better life is being squandered on the altar of self-gratification. The parents, spouse and children of alcoholics don't enjoy them financially and emotionally. May the Lord deliver whoever is already a victim of this in Jesus' name.

UNEMPLOYMENT

Joblessness is also a factor that causes drought-like experience for people the world over. Though joblessness is more pronounced in Africa, the fact remains that it's a common experience in all continents of the world. A jobless man who can't take good care of himself can't raise a family of his own.

Over the years, many of the young criminals arraigned in court in Nigeria often claim they entered into the wicked act out of frustration of joblessness. An idle hand, they say, is the devil's workshop. The drought of joblessness had increased the rate of criminal activities in the world.

It's commonly believed that a man gainfully employed with handsome monthly take-home or someone who chairs a thriving business has thin tendency of being a criminal. But because many of the African youths are jobless, criminal activities and corruption are on rampage in the continent.

May the almighty God put a permanent end to this particular drought in the world in Jesus' name! Do you doubt His ability? What's impossible for man is absolutely possible for God. He calls the things that are not as if they were. He brought visibility to the beginning chaos and emptiness of the world. He had done it before; He would do it again! If you believe say Amen.

SUDDEN AND INCESSANT RETRENCHMENT

This particular factor of drought currently affects at least five percent of the families of the world. The general economic meltdown had led and still leading some nation's government and private industries into reducing their staff strength.

Agreeing with this fact, Ayo Olukotun in his article posted on the Punch Newspaper Site on August 12, 2016 said, "To be sure, job cuts for a variety of reasons are a worldwide trend that is not about to go away. Most of the industrialized countries have had their share of this bitter pill. For example, China, one of the world's strongest economies, is about to embark on massive labour shedding forecast to run into millions in what is projected as the biggest retrenchment programme in 20 years. But that is not the end of the story, for two affected industries, namely the coal and steel sectors, the country has budgeted the equivalent of $23bn in order to ease the woes and fallout of the exercise. In other words, China's version of the developmental state is not one that throws its workers into the bitter cold without providing them with protective garments."

Even in Nigeria, "Next to the saga of ever increasing arrears of salaries owed to workers by close to 30 states, is the anguish of job layoffs across the country, both obviously signs of the upsetting times. Variously described euphemistically as downsizing or rightsizing, the firing of workers across a wide spectrum of the economy has become a frightening marker of the current recession, mitigated in part by the Federal Government's commendable policy of not sacking its employees." Ayo Olukotunadded.

In the world today, there's no day that at least a person is not either fired or relieved of his job. Singapore's second most-read newspaper 'Today', in the article updated onits site on June10, 2016attests that:

"SINGAPORE — Resorts World Sentosa (RWS) is cutting its casino headcount and letting go of close to 400 employees as it struggles against unprecedented headwinds from the retreat of mainly Chinese high rollers due to a combination of a corruption crackdown led by President Xi Jinping and a slowdown in the world's second largest economy. TODAY understands that about 150 croupiers, 200 supervisors and 25 pit managers have been let go in recent weeks, either via voluntary retrenchment or termination of services. A pit manager, who was served his letter on Thursday (June 9) after being with RWS since it opened in 2010, told TODAY, the casino has about 1,400 croupiers, 700 supervisors and 130 pit managers."

That's a pointer to the fact that some families in the world are undergoing the drought of retrenchment. Some families are suffering financially and materially. These families could no longer eat what they like or send their kids to best schools as they had dreamt.

Some husbands have been crippled such that they could no longer financially shower love on their wives because of sudden retrenchment from work. Many dreams of better life had been buried by this particular drought – many drawn architectural edifies remain a plan that can't be materialized. A victim of current sudden retrenchment in Singapore with regret lamented:

> My wife is in terrible shock; she's been crying the whole day … Some of my colleagues had just bought houses. Not even one month yet then this thing happens … The whole resort world casino staff, there is so much stress, they are traumatized, wondering if they will be called up next,(Today Newspaper).

Friend, are you currently passing through this particular drought-like experience? Do you now live below your dreamt standard of life because of retrenchment? Does your wife and children now learn to adjust to a lower class of life than they had been living because daddy was suddenly fired from work?

Have your parents stopped receiving the monthly allowance you usually give them because you're now, so to say, jobless? There's hope for you. Yes, there's a hope for you in Christ Jesus. May the Lord send you help from Zion! May He lift up your head again among your counterparts. May He send you a brand new job that has more benefits than the one you lost in Christ's name! You shall flourish again!

DEBT

This agent of drought had ruined many lives, scattered homes, buried visions, killed ambitions, closed down factories and corporate companies, and has also troubled the tranquility and development of nations. There're many calm and easy-going men that have been turned wild by debt. There're formerly greatly ambitious people that have been turned nothing better than dummy by unexpected liability.

Some homes could no longer sit together to take unanimous decision because of the drought of debt that has eaten them deep. It's even saddening to know that many privately owned factories and corporate companies now run their firm on debt – they currently borrow money from financial houses to sustain their business. Anyway, it's no longer news that a number of nations now borrow to run their usual annual budgets.

Debts have crippled the health of a number of people in the world. Cardiac arrest, high blood pressure and stroke have been sponsored into people's body system through abrupt debt. Accumulated debts have turned some highly intelligent and vibrant business magnates bedridden. I pray that God would visit the lives of those affected by this agent of drought in Jesus' name. May all debt crippled homes, companies and nations receive divine visit that'll revive and restore them in Jesus' name.

WAR AND INSURGENCY

War and insurgency are major, current cause of drought in many nations of the world, especially in Africa and Asia. It's inevitable that any nation experiencing war or insurgency will be financially and materially crippled. People are displaced; some are maimed while others are killed. Properties, publicly and privately owned, are destroyed mercilessly.

Natural resources are vandalized by the insurgents. And when victim-nations eventually have upper hand, they run into unprecedented season of drought. What option do they have then than to depend on charitable materials sent from other nations! I pray that every nation experiencing insurgency or war should receive peace in Jesus' name. Amen!

FAILURE TO SAVE IN THE RAINY DAY

The method of saving in the rainy day for period of drought dated back as early 2700BC. The method was propounded by God through Joseph in Egypt. Joseph having unravelled the meaning of king Pharaoh's dream advised the king to build a tower and appoint a man to store up grains for the land in the years of surplus so that the people may have something to eat in the years of drought. The advice was followed and the land had enough to eat and to also sell to other nations during the seven years of drought (see Genesis 41:34-37).

This principle has not lost its power. Any individual, home and community that fail to save in the rainy day or season will suffer lack in the year of drought. Any nation or institution that refused to save in the year of surplus will languish in want and will even become a debtor in the period of drought. Every individual who desires the best for himself and his home throughout life should embrace the custom of saving his surplus for the possible year of drought.

A nation that desire continuous economic progress and prosperity for her citizens must mark out efficient plan to preserve her surplus. This is also expected of any firm that wants to thrive continuously in the business world. The surplus to preserve ranges from agricultural produce surplus, factory production surplus, income surplus, annual financial budget surplus to natural resources surplus (i.e. crude oil, precious stones, iron ore etc.).

A nation with poor or no preservative plan will be subservient to other nations she ought to lead in the years of drought. Many nations' governments of the world today are victim of this principle, that's why we are experiencing economic recession.

When a government only looks at and concerns herself with today, she definitely will not plan for tomorrow. The whole world today needs leaders that have foresight for tomorrow. Leaders who are ready to save in rainy day to prevent the occurrence of future famine. We need leaders who understand that today's surplus is provision for tomorrow's needs. Many of our leaders are wasters of resources; since they fail to set up workable scheme(s) to preserve the annual surplus of our produces and national incomes.

FLOURISHING IN DROUGHT 1

Thriving during Scarcity is a Miracle – its Achievement is Divine!

Chapter 3
FLOURISHING IN DROUGHT 1

In this chapter we would x-ray the practical principles of flourishing in drought. I would carefully list and examine three basic divine principles that govern thriving during drought. Hence, I implore you to patiently read the revelations in this chapter with a keen heart, taking notice of what is really expected of whoever desires to flourish during drought. This will enable you to key into the practicality of the experience.

REPOSING YOUR TRUST IN GOD

Blessed is the man who trusts in the Lord, and whose hope is the Lord. For he shall be like a tree planted by the waters, which spreads out its roots by the river, and will not fear when heat comes; but its leaf will be green, and will not be anxious in the year of drought, nor will cease from yielding fruit. (Jeremiah 17:7-8)

Here the man – anyone who trusts in God is declared blessed. This simply reveals that putting one's trust in God is a major means of attracting divine blessing on one's life. But, what does putting one's trust in God really means? It means believing in, relying on, having faith in, waiting for and resting one's life on God's word and promises. Trust in God is demonstrated when one keeps believing in His word even when the fulfillment of His promise seems delayed.

Why is the man who trusts in God blessed? God intentionally bless whoever trusts in Him upon two major reasons. First, trusting in Him agrees with the type of life He designed man to live. The life God designed for man is dependent from the beginning to the end. Man's life was not designed to be lived independent of God. We were originally created to cleave to God. We are then expected to hook-up our lives on Him.

He's the vine, we are His branches. God doesn't need us to exist, but we need Him. In Him we live, move and have our being. His Life gives us life. All what we may need throughout our pilgrimage on earth are treasured in Him. Sequel to this, we should glue, cement and permanently attach our individual lives to Him. The foregoing established that God is interested in raining His blessing on whoever puts his trust in Him; because doing so agrees with his eternal plan for man.

Second, God declared whoever puts his trust in Him blessed because dissociating oneself from Him introduces one's life to a season of spiritual and physical dryness. The beauty of man's life lies in his ability to glue himself to God. When a man tries to dissociate himself from or decide not to repose his trust in God, he'll suffer dryness in all areas of his life. Dryness will be evident in his spiritual, academic, professional, health, finance, material, ministerial, marital … aspect of life. When this happens, the person's life will be completely barren – productivity will be far from him.

Those who decide neither to repose their trust in God nor associate themselves with Him are on the verge of sacrificing the fulfillment of their destiny. This is because without God you can do but nothing. The dangers of dissociating yourself from God or removing your trust from Him are disastrous! To worsen the whole matter, whoever refused to repose his trust in God continually will definitely not make eternity with Him. Such a life will rot in hell.

Having carefully examined the implication of reposing one's trust in God and why God declared whoever puts his or her trust in Him blessed. We then need to examine when actually can a man put his trust in God? What really can happen to a man that will make him to confidently repose his trust in God continually? Or does it mean it's easy or possible for just anyone to truly repose his trust in God?

Without doubt, realistic evidence proves that reposing one's trust in God isn't something natural for everyone. Those who put their trust in God today had had an experience that enables them to do so yesterday. What then is that experience? What exactly are the things that enable one to continually repose his trust in God? That we would go into straight away.

1. **You Must Hear About God.** That exactly is what is happening to you right now. You necessarily need to hear about God; for faith comes by hearing and hearing by the word of God (see Roman 10:17). You can't believe in whom you haven't heard about. Someone has to talk to you about God.

   At least a person or a written material has to introduce God to you. This is the beginning of putting your trust in God. Hearing about God is basic and foundational in the journey of reposing your trust in Him. Meanwhile, hearing about God will prepare you for the next step, which has to do with believing in Him.

2. **You Must Believe in God.** Your hearing about God prepares you for conviction, repentance and confession. But these can't happen until you had believed in Him. You had to believe what you have heard about God.

When you believe the message shared with you about God, your heart will be convicted of your sinful life; you'll repent of your sins, confess them all to God and forsake the further commission of such sins. The fact is, you can't put your trust in whom you don't believe in (see Romans 10:9-11). When the said experience happens to you, you're getting ready for the last step, which is knowledge.

3. **You Must Know God.** The third thing that enables one to permanently put his trust in God is knowledge. Yes, knowledge of whom He is. The true knowledge of who God is and what He can do is an enabling factor that moves people to confidently repose their trust in Him. The fact is, you can't trust whom you don't know.

If a stranger just walk up to you to promise you a thing, would you ever believe his word? I think, no. You won't believe him because you don't know him. You don't know his person, ability, position, influence and affluence.

The matter is same in the kingdom. No matter how you claim to have known the Bible, you'll find it difficult to repose your trust in God when you didn't personally know Him experientially. Many have head-knowledge of the Bible to the extent that they can even quote several of its verses off hand, but they don't know the God of the Bible.

It's possible for anyone to be familiar with the stories of the Bible; for Bible is an open book, which anyone can buy in bookshop and read. The truth is, whoever doesn't know God experientially can't repose his trust in Him. A principal condition in putting one's trust in God is acquiring His knowledge. This simply implies you can't trust Him if you don't know Him. Knowing Him opens you to trusting Him.

The level at which you know Him is the degree at which you can trust Him. You can't trust God beyond how much you know Him! Sequel to this realization, if you desire to trust God you must also prepare to know Him.

A genuine thirst for His knowledge has to erupt and daily increase in you. You need to desperately pursue the knowledge of His person, power, likes and dislikes, grace, sovereignty, authority, creativity, awesomeness etc. You need to know Him as Jehovah Jireh, before you can trust Him as your provider.

Even if anyone testifies of God's providential power to you, it'll make no sense to you till you personally know and miraculously encounter Him that way. It'll be completely impossible for you to believe God for your life protection if you haven't practically known Him as the true defender. No matter how you read the scriptures, you'll not be able to trust God for your healing spiritually and physically, if you haven't known and encountered Him as Jehovah Raphael.

The vital springboard of trust is knowledge. Even in marriage and business, trust is unachievable without knowledge. At least, there must be right knowledge of the parties involved. Little wonder Paul, one the famous early apostle made knowing Christ the continuous pursuit of his life. He publicly declared:

"I want to know Christ and the power of his resurrection and the fellowship of sharing in his sufferings, becoming like him in his death," (Philippians 3:10 NIV). Knowing God should be a continuous pursuit of whoever desires to trust Him. Knowing Him progressively will result to trusting in Him regularly and unendingly. The yardstick to determine the level at which you trust God is the degree of His knowledge you have.

But you need to know that the earlier you put your trust in God, the sooner your life will be better. Also, the frequent you trust God, the recurrent the fulfillment you'll record in your lifetime. Hence, you should learn to trust God by pursuing His knowledge progressively. I hope you get that right.

Let's now proceed into viewing the picture of how the life of whoever reposes his trust in God would be. Under this we are to x-ray the outcome or benefits of reposing one's life trust in God. All I've been explaining from the first paragraph of this chapter is to bring you into the potency of reposing your trust continually in God. Consequently, I implore you to patiently follow me on as we draw more from the well of Life.

Outcome of Reposing Your Trust in God

> ***Blessed is the man who trusts in the Lord, and whose hope is the Lord.***
>
> ***For he shall be like a tree planted by the waters, which spreads out its roots by the river, and will not fear when heat comes; but its leaf will be green, and will not be anxious in the year of drought, nor will cease from yielding fruit.*** (Jeremiah 17:7-8)

Whoever dares to continually repose his trust in God will "**Flourish in Drought.**" *"For he shall be like a tree planted by the waters, which spreads out its roots by the river, and will not fear when heat comes; but its leaf will be green, and will not be anxious in the year of drought."*

The life of whoever puts his trust in God continually will be like a tree planted by the waters, which spread its roots by the river. Such life will neither fear nor be anxious when financial, material, health … heat comes. His life, home, career and spiritual life will be evergreen.

Such men are not usually anxious in the year of drought – since they had reposed their trust in the unfailing providential power and promises of God. When other men are languishing in want, such a man can't because his provision comes from the Most-high God. His provisions are channeled by celestial hand and not terrestrial. His fortune flows from the eternal bolt, hence he can't go bankrupt. God's own purse is inexhaustible – His treasury can't run out of provision – He has all things in abundance.

This was what David was expressing by saying, *"The Lord is my shepherd, I shall not want…"* (Psalms 23)

Others' spiritual life, finance, progress, productivity, establishment and advancement may be melted during global or national economic meltdown, but the man who trusts in God will keep on flourishing. God's word says he will flourish in the midst of drought. He'll soar during storms – he'll experience peace in the midst storm. Later in this book we'll raise practical examples of people who trusted in God and really experienced the fulfillment of this divine promise.

Furthermore, whoever repose his trust in God will be experiencing year round fruitfulness. "...***nor will cease from yielding fruit.***" (Jeremiah 17:8b) The Bible established that the life of whoever repose his trust in God will not cease yielding fruit. His fruitfulness will not know season – he'll never cast his young. Continuous fruitfulness will be evident in his life, home, career, ministry, academics etc. Whoever repose his trust in God will bear fruit even in his old age.

What can really stop such a man from bearing fruit of souls, advancement, fulfillment, establishment, promotion, victory … is if he stops reposing his trust in God. Those who continually repose their trust in God are destined for and can be obviously identified by continuous fruitfulness, productivity and growth.

LIVING A RIGHTEOUS LIFE

> ***The righteous shall flourish like a palm tree, he shall grow like a cedar in Lebanon.*** Psalms 92:12

This is the second principle that makes a man flourish during drought. In the above quoted scripture, God in his sovereignty declared that the righteous shall flourish like Palm tree and he will grow like cedar in Lebanon. The Palm tree is an evergreen tree among all other trees.

Every other tree may die during drought because they are made of shallow root, but the Palm tree will still be green and fruitful because its taproot travels deep down to the lowest waterbed. The long taproot of Palm tree draws water for it from the lowest waterbed during drought, and that enables it to survive and even flourish during summer.

God compared the flourishing of the righteous to that of the Palm tree to let us know that the righteous has capacity to flourish and grow big in drought just like the Palm tree would do during summer. It's to let us know that just like the Palm tree can't be killed by dryness, so the righteous also are destined and are capable of flourishing during drought.

Hence, the righteous' prosperity is not expected to be seasonal, but all year round. He should flourish, global and national economic situation notwithstanding. His life should be a practical demonstration of the ability of God. His growth, development and advancement should defy natural laws and shock natural men's wisdom and calculations.

Then, who is the righteous? Or what does it mean to be righteous? Being righteous simply means living according to the principles of the word of God after one is washed by the blood of Jesus at repentance. It connotes, making the word of God the standard that guides and guard your life after you have received forgiveness of sin from Jesus.

It implies obeying the scripture, having known what it says. You're righteous when you're addicted to living your life according to the teachings of the word. Such that when your life is juxtaposed with the truth of God's word, there will be no point of disparity between your life and the scriptures. Your life should agree with God's principle of salvation, sanctification, consecration, marriage, business, profession … if you'll be righteous.

BEING PLANTED IN GOD'S PRESENCE

> *Those who are planted in the house of the Lord shall flourish in the courts of our God.*
>
> *They shall still bear fruit in old age; they shall be fresh and flourishing,* Psalms 92:13-14

The third principle that governs flourishing during drought is to be planted in God presence. This implies receiving a resident permit in God's courts. It connotes becoming a resident of God's presence. When a man dwells in God's presence, he contacts divine ability to flourish in drought. God will daily load such a man with wisdom, awesome ideas and creative innovations that'll make him outrageously flourish during the period of drought. But who can really dwell in God's presence?

"… He whose walk is blameless and who does what is righteous, who speaks the truth from his heart and has no slander on his tongue, who does his neighbor no wrong and casts no slur on his fellowman, who despises a vile man but honors those who fear the Lord, who keeps his oath even when it hurts, who lends his money without usury and does not accept a bribe against the innocent. He who does these things will never be shaken."(Psalms 15:1-5)

All that you ever needed in life are planted in God's presence. The earlier you believe this simple truth the sooner your life begins to make sense. The wife, husband, children, job, promotion, prosperity, fulfilment and enlargement … you desire are fully obtainable in His presence. There is nothing you can amount to without God. He is the True Vine; you are His branch – you are destined to receive all your life's needs from Him.

What you need do is to just glue yourself to Him. A man receives nothing unless it is given to Him from above. Your help is from above, not from abroad. Unless the Lord builds a house, the builders' work is useless. Unless the Lord protects a city, patrols and watchmen do no good. It is senseless for you to work so hard from early morning until late at night, fearing you will starve to death…. (See Psalms 127:1-2)

Your life needs are obtainable within the circumference of God's presence. When God led Israel through the wilderness where they could neither sow nor harvest, He was there to supply all their needs. He didn't abandon them to go through the desert alone, He daily walked with them through the ordeal and make sure they didn't lack anything good. He daily rained down manna for them within the circumference of His presence – the manna daily falls within the perimeter of the pillar of cloud and the pillar of fire (see Exodus 16:13-22).

This implies any Israelite who either pitches his tent outside God's divine presence or walk away from His presence when the manna is being dropped misses his daily provision. As many who remain within the confine of God's presence in the wilderness got their daily needs met – you can't live in God's presence and grow lean. Fulfilment, joy, prosperity, expansion… awaits you in God's presence – go right away and pitch your life's tent there!

That's the conditions of becoming a resident of God's presence. When you do the above, you'll be granted access to God's presence. Meeting the conditions look like an uphill task? Jesus has simplified it for us. When you permit Him to dwell in you, He will enable you to fulfill the conditions without stress. Christ in you is the hope of realizing the conditions. (See Colossians 1:27).

FLOURISHING IN DROUGHT 2

Blossoming during Famine is certain when Divine Principles are obeyed!

Chapter 4
FLOURISHING IN DROUGHT 2

***Guard your heart above all else, for it determines the course of your life.**(Proverbs 4:23 NLT)*

DEVELOP A POSITIVE THOUGHT LIFE

Having reposed your trust in God, your thought should be positive about what you currently experience. I need to state early to you that the first place to prove your trust in God is your heart. Your thought should become positive despite what you are currently experiencing. The positive change, breakthrough … you desire need to begin with your thought.

Until you experience change of thought you can't experience a positive dramatic change in your life. Your current predicament is tied to your thought just as your breakthrough is. You are product of your thought.

Your life can't be better than how your thought is. Your life is a perfect reflection of the state of your thought. The liberation you need from the current mess you are has to begin with your thought. Till your thought is liberated your life can't experience any form of liberation.

There are hundreds of people that God could have helped out of their life's predicaments, but who's thought continually prevent divine help from reaching them. God can't break His principle. As a man thinks in his heart so is he (see Proverbs 23:7). When you want to get out of a drought-like experience, your thought should show you believe you'll be out of it one day.

Faith is having the substance – apparent evidence of what you hope for first in your heart – in your thought even when it hasn't come in physically (see Hebrews 11:1). Your thought should prove you are not resigning to fate. Prayer can't help any man who silently resigns to fate at his thought level. Some people even need thought deliverance before they can experience practical emancipation in their life.

You can develop positive thought life by filling your heart with the word of God. Meditate daily on God's promises instead of concentrating your thought on your life situation. The more you feed on the words of God the more you think about the word. Concentrating your thought on your circumstance will expose you to depression and anxiety; while concentrating it on the word will eliminate your burdens and give you hope for better tomorrow.

Are you currently having a drought-like experience in your life? Is your home going through a season of drought? Or your nation is having her share of the current global economic drought? Think positively about it! Don't permit the situation to force you into resigning to fate that the hope of better tomorrow is completely lost. Fill your heart with the word of God. Think about God's promises – that's enough to make you a conqueror at your thought level. Stop thinking negative about the situation.

SPEAK POSITIVE WORD

> ***Avoid all perverse talk; stay away from corrupt speech.*** Proverbs 4:24

When your thought is positive, your word is expected to be positive. This is because man's words spring out of his thought. If you really repose your trust in God and you think positively about your current experience, there should be a proof of this in your word. When you find yourself in a drought-like experience, you need to profess something positive about your life not negative.

When your business no longer yields profit as it use to, don't speak negative word about it – words are spirits, they have a way of influencing our lives, homes and whatever we do. You also need to speak positively about the current economic and political situation of your nation. As a good citizen who repose his trust continually in God, negative word shouldn't proceed from your mouth. Your words shouldn't be negative about your nation no matter what happens.

When Israel traveled through the wilderness, God promised to take them to a land flowing with milk and honey. When they were very close to the Promised Land some of them doubted and spoke negatively about God's promise.

This was the content of their words *"If only we had died in Egypt! Or in this desert! Why is the Lord bringing us to this land only to let us fall by the sword? Our wives and children will be taken as plunder. Wouldn't it be better for us to go back to Egypt?" And they said to each other, "We should choose a leader and go back to Egypt.""*(Numbers 14:2-4NIV) Later, God pronounced judgment on them out of His indignation:

"As surely as I live, declares the Lord, I will do to you the very things I heard you say: In this desert your bodies will fall — every one of you twenty years old or more who was counted in the census and who has grumbled against me. Not one of you will enter the land I swore with uplifted hand to make your home, except Caleb son of Jephunneh and Joshua son of Nun. As for your children that you said would be taken as plunder, I will bring them in to enjoy the land you have rejected. But you — your bodies will fall in this desert. Your children will be shepherds here for forty years, suffering for your unfaithfulness, until the last of your bodies lies in the desert. For forty years — one year for each of the forty days you explored the land — you will suffer for your sins and know what it is like to have me against you.' I, the Lord, have spoken, and I will surely do these things to this whole wicked community, which has banded together against me. They will meet their end in this desert; here they will die."(Numbers 14:28-35NIV)

If you carefully read the punishment God declared on the Israelites as relayed above, you will note that they were judged according to their words. What they said with their mouth was what God offered to them. All of those men died in the wilderness because they professed that they will die. Meanwhile, their words steamed out of doubt and fear.

Don't doubt what God had promised to do in your life, home, business, profession, academics and country. Instead of entertaining doubt, profess the promises of God to your life, home, business and nation. Others may profess negativity about your nation; you should learn to speak positively. As you are saying it, God hears you and He will perform those words.

Instead of professing negative words about your nation, you are expected to pray. It is written, ***"Pray for the peace of Jerusalem: May they prosper who love you. Peace be within your walls, prosperity within your palaces. For the sake of my brethren and companions, I will now say, Peace be within you. Because of the house of the Lord our God I will seek your good."***(Psalms 122:6-9)

Your nation is your Jerusalem – pray for her peace and progress. Drop the idea of shifting blame on leaders, try and pray – perform your own quota and you shall be blessed for doing so. According to the above scripture, your prosperity is directly attached to your readiness and ability to pray for the peace and progress of your nation. When you refuse to pray, your prosperity both within and outside that nation will be hindered. That will not be your experience in Jesus' name.

The bitter truth is, we all need to pray for the peace and progress of our nation(s) not only during economic recession but as long as there is breath in us. We are to pray for our leaders and the governance of our nation. Things remain how it is because you have not prayed. Try praying from today – profess positive word about your life, home and your nation. Say something like this:

> ***Though I walk in the midst of trouble, You will revive me; You will stretch out your hand against the wrath of my enemies, and Your right hand will save me. The Lord will perfect that which concerns me; your mercy, O Lord, endures forever; do not forsake the works of your hands.***
>
> ***The Lord is my shepherd, I shall not be in want. He makes me lie down in green pastures, he leads me beside quiet waters, he restores my soul. He guides me in paths of righteousness for his name's sake. Even though I walk through the valley of the shadow of death, I will fear no evil, for you are with me; your rod and your staff, they comfort me. You prepare a table before me in the presence of my enemies. You anoint my head with oil; my cup overflows. Surely goodness and love will follow me all the days of my life, and I will dwell in the house of the Lord forever.*** (Psalms 138:7-8Psalms 23:1-6)

EXHIBIT POSITIVE ACTIONS

The fact that you trust in God, think and speak positively should reflect in your actions. Negative action whether against yourself, your home, business or nation will only worsen the situation of things. Negative action can never produce positive result.

If you desire positive change in your life, your action towards yourself and decisions you make should be positive too. Even if it is in your home that you desire positive transformation, productivity and expansion, your actions and decisions within and towards the home should be positive; so the desired change might be rendered.

Don't behave negatively toward the members of your family – two wrongs can't produce anything positive (i.e. $-2+-2=-4$). Is the economy of your nation experiencing a downturn and you believe God for positive change, transformation and progress, your action toward the nation should also be positive! Your positive actions and contributions will be your own donation to the development of your nation. Don't let the hard situation push you to act negatively in and toward your nation.

Don't behave like someone who doesn't have hope of restoration! All hope is not lost; things shall be better soon – be yourself – behave as a righteous person. Always remember, as a man thinks in his heart so he is – as a man thinks so he acts and behaves. Your action toward yourself, home, community and nation in hard times is an un-doubtable reflection of your thoughts about the situation. Then watch your thought, for that is the bedrock of your actions. A positive thought will produce positive action.

DON'T GAMBLE, ASK GOD FOR SPECIFIC SOLUTION

> *There are many plans in a man's heart, nevertheless the Lord's counsel — that will stand.* Proverbs 19:21

When hard situation comes just like the current global economic recession, individuals and even nation leaders tend to gamble. When pressure increases on men, it usually produces tension. Where there is tension, coordination and competence is usually at zero level. At such a period it is impossible to think straight. Hence, the easiest thing to do during difficult times is to gamble. During hard times men tend to apply try and error approach on issues, whereas they need specific guidance at such a time. Applying try and error approach on issues at a time when productive decisions are expected to be made in a home, community and a nation may create more damages than supplying needed solution.

Sequel to the above summation, in times of economic downturn, I need to counsel you, dear friend that you need not gamble with your life. You don't need try and error approach in sensitive times. You rather need to go to God about your life and home.

Specifically ask Him for the exact thing you can do that will produce the solution – the particular type of financial breakthrough that your life and home need. God has solution to whatever type of drought you are experiencing, whether spiritual, academic, financial, psychological…. The good news is, He is ready to instruct and guide whoever dares to consult Him. Read His commitment to you:

> ***I will instruct you (says the Lord) and guide you along the best pathway for your life; I will advise you and watch your progress.***
>
> ***Don't be like a senseless horse or mule that has to have a bit in its mouth to keep it in line!*** Psalms 32:8-9 TLB

Do you hear God saying "I will instruct you … guide you along the best pathway for your life; I will advise you and watch your progress?" Your progress in life and home is God's interest. He said I will ensure and supervise your progress.

Meanwhile, this will only happen when you dare to ask Him for direction, instruction and advice in critical times. That's why He said *"Don't be like a senseless horse or mule that has to have a bit in its mouth to keep it in line!"* in the concluding part of the above scripture. When you ask Him for direction, you are also expected to obey whatever He leads you to do. According to the above passage when you disobey His instruction you are acting like an animal.

You are not expected to edit God's direction to you by your own common sense. He is all wise – He knows what He asks you to do will produce the desired result. The truth is, many at times God's direction usually appears foolish to human common sense. But those who trusted Him in the past neither doubt nor edit any of His direction in their pilgrimage.

God is the unchangeable changer – He changes situations and circumstances while He remains constant. He enthrones and dethrones kings and rulers; there is no one to query Him. He solves riddles and give meaning to enigma – He is the solution to all man's perditions (see Daniel 2:47).

He specializes in making impossibility possible. Whatever seems impossible for humans – whatever human discretion judged impossible is absolutely possible with God. He's been doing this since the time of creation – He brought creative creations out of emptiness and nothingness. (See Genesis 1:1-31)

Some centuries ago in Israel, a widow of a prophet found herself in the state of penury. Her deceased husband instead of leaving fortune for her and her children left a huge debt for them to pay. In the meantime, the creditor threatened to take her two sons as slaves, just because they couldn't settle the debt. Then, the woman cried out to God through Prophet Elisha.

The prophet gave her specific instruction of what to do and she followed the instruction to detail. That same day the woman's story and status changed. She became so blessed financially that she had enough money to settle the debt and to live in luxury afterward (see 2 Kings 4:1-7).

The God of heavens and earth is a miracle Worker; whatever His hand touches usually experience a turn around. I assure you a dramatic change if you dare to consult Him for exact solution to the prevailing challenges of your life, home, business, profession.... If you will do what the widow did, you'll be in for a miracle.

My dear reader, solution awaits you in Christ Jesus. There is no point continuing in that sorrow and hardship. Humble yourself, go to God and ask Him for the exact solution to your challenge. Let Him tell you the exact thing you can do to turn the tide of your life experience.

He never fails – He can't miss the target – when He tells you what to do there is assurance that you can't regret it. Receiving from Him and following His instruction to detail pedestals for divine miracle. You shall surely share testimony if you can truly trust Him. Since this opportunity is available, why gambling?

Similarly, national leaders are to also glean wisdom from this same matter. You don't need to gamble or make use of try and error approach on national decisions at this crucial time. Your citizens look up to you for correct decisions that will bring dramatic economical change which our land need. Gambling at decisions in this kind of time will make you appear foolish, indecisive and unguided before the citizens.

You need to know that you are elected there as a game changer, hence, you should be exact in your decisions. This is the kind of time you are to prove your capability in leadership. The solution to the current confusion should come through you. However, you neither need to gamble nor rush at making decisions; your citizens will be disappointed and become indispose to you should your methods fail.

In the first instance, you need to know and acknowledge the truth in this word of wisdom: ***"… mere mortals can't run their own lives … men and women don't have what it takes to take charge of life."*** (see Jeremiah 10:23) As a nation leader, you need to acknowledge that it is not within the power of man to map his life and plan his course. Despite that you are in the helm of the affairs of your nation, you should know that it is not within your power to plan the course of things without acknowledging God. You are not expected to take the law into your own hands, concluding that you can run the government, take decisions, and constitute committees… only in your own wisdom.

God is the King of kings, the Lord of rulers; any leader or ruler that thinks he can govern without acknowledging Him plan to have a futile tenure. The truth remains that whatever He decides not to do would remainunaccomplished for any leader. A leader who desires productive and successful tenure must depend on Him. Such a leader will patiently consult and receive from God before making his own plans and decisions. Why many contemporary political leaders of nations are not making realistic productive headway in their governance is majorly because they had turned against God. They pitched the tent of their lives and government separate from the King of kings – that's why they lack His support.

I desire you glean wisdom from some kings in history who depended and submitted to God in their time and set records that are difficult to match. David Jesse the second king of Israel was appointed by God and depended solely on Him throughout his reign. He came to reign over Israel when there were many battles to fight and just because he depended on God he didn't lose any till his death.

History bears it that he usually consults God for direction before taking a step or wages a battle (see 1 Samuel 23:2-5, 30:1-31, 2 Samuel 5:17-25). He gained prominence throughout the then world, made Israel wealthy, grew old on the throne, appointed his successor and instruct him to walk with God before he finally died (see 1 Kings 1:32-40, 2:2-4). David is referenced as a good ruler in Israel till today.

Nebuchadnezzar of Babylon who reigned around 6th century B.C. neither know nor acknowledged God initially till he invaded Jerusalem and brought some Jews captives to his land. His empire was so great then that he had world power.

But pride entered his heart and said, *"Is not this great Babylon that I have built for a royal dwelling by my mighty power and for the honour of my majesty?"* While he was yet spilling the unruly words from his mouth, God decided to teach him a lesson he will never forget in his whole life's time.

He took his reasoning from him, drove him away from the vicinity of men to go and dwell in the wilderness for seven full years. He ate grass like oxen; his body was wet with the dew till his hair grew like eagles' feathers and his nails like birds' claws. He dwelt with the beasts till he acknowledged God and repented of his pride. Read the account of his personal testimony from Daniel chapter four. May your own not go to that point before you will acknowledge and submit to God.

Consequently, I counsel you to consult God for what to do to solve the riddle of the current economic challenge instead of consulting men or books. You are to resort to God for specific instruction of what to do in this kind of time. God is the supreme game changer who can be absolutely trusted. Every leader that would make headway in his governance must submit to God. Such a leader should be ready to walk with God in His own terms.

Many decades ago, Pharaoh of Egypt trusted the living God, consulted Him about his nation, followed His counsel and his nation was preserved from the seven years of famine that struck the land (see Genesis 41:1-55). The famine was so severe and spread across all the nations on the surface of the earth, but Egypt had more than enough food to eat and to sell to people of other nations just because Pharaoh believed in and consulted God.

For those seven years, Egypt fed nations from her abundance (see Genesis 41:56-57). If you also would consult God about whatever crisis your country is experiencing, He will tell you what to do to bring a turnaround in your land.

Ben-Hadad king of Syria besieged Samaria some centuries ago, paving way for great famine in the land. The famine was so severe that women killed, boiled their children and ate them for survival. When it got to an acute point, Elisha the prophet consulted God on behalf of the land and God gave them the promise of twenty-four hours' miracle. This was the content of the promise: ***"Hear the word of the LORD. Thus says the Lord: 'Tomorrow about this time a seah of fine flour shall be sold for a shekel, and two seahs of barley for a shekel at the gate of Samaria."***

Just as God promised the miracle happened – abundance came to Samaria within twenty-four hours. The severe famine came to an end in the land when God stepped into their case (see 2 Kings 6:24-33, 7: 1-20). The king's officer who doubted the fulfillment of the promise was trampled to death at the gate of the city when the promise was fulfilled.

God is the supreme game changer – change is certain whenever He steps into a situation. The world would experience positive change in her economies if world leaders would consult God on behalf of their nations. This is so important because God doesn't intervene in issues until He is deliberately consulted and invited. If you can consult Him about your nation, your citizens could experience peace and prosperity sooner than any other nation in the world.

The sooner you yield to Him, the earlier you have solution to the challenge. When you consult Him, He will give you a creative idea or step that will terminate the current unbearable suffering. Would you be so humble to consult Him? Would pride of your heart not keep your citizens in long season of drought and suffering? If you will not even go to God because of yourself, I beg you to go because of your citizens. May the dear Lord grant us help soon!

SOW IN THE DIFFICULT TIMES

> ***Give, and it will be given to you. A good measure, pressed down, shaken together and running over, will be poured into your lap. For with the measure you use, it will be measured to you.*** Luke 6:38 NIV

Whenever the issue of flourishing in drought is being discussed, the principle of sowing and reaping shouldn't be overlooked. Yes, many people believe this principle and practice it only when things are rosy. The current global economic challenge had made some adherents of the principle to decline from giving. Many people who were known as givers – helpers of the needy had stopped giving, claiming that themselves don't have enough to attend to their own needs and feed their homes.

However, everyone needs to know that the principle of sowing and reaping didn't only apply in the raining day – it also applies in the difficult times. If there is any best time to sow seeds of giving, it is during the hard times. Yes, you may not have much, but you can still remove a seed to sow into people's life, God's kingdom business or His servant's life from the little you have.

Don't let the current economic downturn turn you stingy. Keep in mind that there is a seed to sow, no matter how little, in whatever blessing you receive from God. The Scripture says, ***"Those who sow in tears shall reap in joy. He who continually goes forth weeping, bearing seed for sowing, shall doubtless come again with rejoicing, bringing his sheaves with him."*** (Ps. 126:5-6) Note in the above scripture that whoever dares to sow in tears – in difficult and hard times shall definitely reap in joy.

He who continually goes forth weeping as he sows, shall doubtlessly come back with rejoicing, bringing in his sheaves. The time to do just that is now! There should be continuity in your giving, that's why the Bible says, ***"He who continually goes forth…."*** Giving in difficult times is a way to flourish during famine. Remember, the widow of Sarephath sowed her last meal during famine and she reaped in multiple folds (see 1 Kings 17:8-24).

Sequel to the above, I challenge you to give generously, for your gifts will return to you later. Divide your gifts among many, for in the days ahead you yourself may need much help. When the clouds are heavy, the rains come down; when a tree falls, whether south or north, the die is cast, for there it lies. If you wait for perfect conditions, you will never get anything done. God's ways are as mysterious as the pathway of the wind and as the manner in which a human spirit is infused into the little body of a baby while it is yet in its mother's womb. Keep on sowing your seed, for you never know which will grow – perhapsit all will (see Eccl. 11:1-6 TLB).

FOLLOW HIS INSTRUCTION

Don't be too wise in your own sight as to edit whatever instruction God gives you. Once He speaks to you, you are expected to obey Him to letter. Divine blessing lies in complete obedience. If you fail to follow His leading the desired change will be hindered.

Realizing the above truths, the subsequent chapters will be practical. We would begin to examine examples of men whose lives proved and affirmed the studied truths. I mean men who practically flourished in the year of drought in their nations and even in foreign lands just because they met the discussed conditions.

Again, the conditions are: Reposing One's Trust in God, Living a Righteous Life, Being Planted in God's Presence, Developing Positive Thought, Speaking Positive Words, Receiving Specific Divine Guidance and Acting According the Received Guidance.

Going through their catalog will confirm to you that the Bible principles taught in this book is true. It's possible to flourish in drought, if one continually trusts in God, live holy life, become a resident of God's presence and obey the rest rules.

FROM BEREAVEMENT AND CAPTIVITY TO ROYALTY

Catastrophe is not the End of Life – It's the Making Process that prepares you for Manifestation!

Chapter 5
FROM BEREAVEMENT AND CAPTIVITY TO ROYALTY

While meditating about men who flourished during the period of drought, the story of Esther and Mordecai came to mind. Because they trust and feared God, these two Hebrews flourished where and in the period they ought to be barren. The secret of their flourishing in drought was nothing else than their trust in God. They believed in the God of their fathers, feared Him, obeyed Him and repose their trust permanently in Him.

Esther Flourished inDrought

First, she had drought of loss of parents. Esther lost both parents when she was young.Becoming an orphan, she was hopeless and stranded. Imagine what condition a young girl who is bereaved of her both parents would be. It was as though her world had crashed. She was destitute of parental love, care, warmth, protection etc. Such a girl just has to voluntarily withdraw from school since there is no one to pay her fees. All parent's occasional gifts, comforts and encouragements ceased.

Nevertheless, divine help located her. Her uncle, Mordecai picked her up and nursed her as his own daughter (see Esther 2:7). Esther like some contemporary young girls could have decided to go the wrong way because of her predicament, but she didn't because she trusted in God – she reposed her trust completely in God. Without doubt, her trust in God was what eventually raised her up above her drought of bereavement.

Come to think of it, Mordecai could have ignored Esther just like many relative of orphans and widows usually do in the current time. But he acted otherwise. One may then ask, what really steered Mordecai to bring Esther up as his own? Could it be God? Yes, it could really be God because the story in the book of Esther shows that Mordecai knew, walked with and feared God. The fact that Esther repose her trust in God could have moved Him to steer Mordecai to rescue her from the bitter situation she suddenly found herself.

Dear reader, are you bereaved? Have you lost one or both of your parents? Or you've lost an uncle, aunt or somebody dear and of great support to you and you're already thinking your world had crashed. Are you already thinking an end has come to your progress and fulfillment in life because you lost your helper to death? I have good news for you!

You don't have to give up. You don't have to put full stop where God puts a comma. God who raised helpers for Esther will raise helpers for you. Your life, home, future and vision will not crash-land. God will raise destiny helpers from where you least expect in Jesus' name. Divine help is coming your way already. Just believe and trust in God. Your predicament will soon become a raw material with which God will produce a miracle.

Another situation of drought came up later in the story, and that was of captivity. This particular drought-like situation happened to both Esther and Mordecai. Both the helped and the helper were carried to captivity. They became captives under King Ahasuerus (see Esther 2:5-7).

As captives, they lived regimented life according to the directives of their captor. I believe you know that captivity is not a sweet experience. The period a man spends in whatever type of captivity is a season of drought, un-productivity and stagnation.

But against all odds, Esther and Mordecai rose to prominence. They practically rose from bereavement and captivity into royalty miraculously. Meanwhile, this doesn't happen to them by chance, their trust in the God of their fathers and persistence in keeping their godly consecration earned them the unique experience.

It's practically difficult to believe that a captive young lady could rise to become the favoured queen of her captor (see Esther 2:15-18). Also, that a regimented Mordecai could become second in command in the whole empire of Ahasuerus, which spread from India to Ethiopia – a hundred and twenty-seven provinces in all (see Esther 8:15, 10:3).

But their trust in God and consistency in righteous living made it possible. God will make impossibility possible in your life if you can continuously live a righteous life and repose your trust in Him.

The righteous who decides to go on trusting in God will experience numerous miracles in their lives as they continue their pilgrimage on earth. God is always jealous for those who completely repose their trust in Him. The challenges in your life, home, business or profession doesn't come to mar you, but to make you. Life challenges are instrument in God's hand to prepare and make His children ready for the fulfillment of their life purposes.

More often than not God uses difficult situations to perfect the making of His children. Those life challenges you face are to perfect you for the platform of manifestation God had made for you. This is to prevent you from getting to your generation without being groomed. Sequel to this understanding, learn to repose your trust in God while passing through life difficulties and challenges.

Little did Esther know that bereavement and captivity were making process for her! Imagine, she wouldn't have been brought up by Mordecai if she was not bereaved of her parents.

Also, it would have been practically difficult or even impossible for her to rise up into risking her life for the Jews in the land whom Haman had determined to wipe out if she hadn't experienced the pain of losing a loved one (see Esther 4:15-17). Likewise, the destiny of been a favoured queen in a strange land would have eluded her if she had escaped the captivity. You actually need to think it through, dear reader.

Besides, Mordecai could have also missed the opportunity of standing for God in a strange land if he had escaped the captivity. He could have lost the chance of being the queen's father in his life time if he had refused to pick nurture Esther as his own. Without doubt, he couldn't have been second in command in that big empire if he had refused to stick out his neck during Haman's determined persecution.

In it all, I need to remind you that the trust Esther and Mordecai had in God was the springboard for their manifestation. Dare to trust in God even when challenges stares at you; you can flourish in drought. Your life can bud and blossom during drought-like season of situation. But this will happen when you make concerted effort to be righteous and continually repose your trust in God.

FROM ADVERSITY TO RULERSHIP

Hard Times Doesn't Come to break you – It Comes to make you!

Chapter 6
FROM ADVERSITY TO RULERSHIP
Another man who literally flourished in drought was Joseph. The man Joseph had a long season of drought-like experiences. His season of drought starts from when he was about seventeen years old boy and it continued consistently until he was thirty years old. He had about thirteen years of continuous drought-like experiences. But in it all God vindicated him and he flourished because he reposed his trust in God. Those who puts their trust in God shall never be put to shame, says the scripture.

DROUGHT-LIKE EXPERIENCE IN JOSEPH'S LIFE

Hatred: The fear of the Lord had been in Joseph's heart since he was young. The Bible attests that he usually reports the misdeeds of his elder brothers to their father. And for this, they hated him so much. It would have been impossible for Joseph to report the misdeeds of his brothers if he was bad fellow like them. Likewise, his father wouldn't have believed his reports if he couldn't vouch for his integrity. Just because Joseph wished his brothers a better life, they hated him (see Genesis 37:2).

Not only that, they also hated him because their father loved him more than them. Jacob specially loved Joseph because he was the son of his old age (see Genesis 37:3-4). His brothers couldn't figure out why their father loved Joseph more than he loved them; they hated him. Beside all the above mentioned reasons, Joseph was also hated because of his dreams.

His dreams of being great to the extent that his parents and brother will come and prostrate to him - his dreams of the great future made him to have more enemies than friends (see Genesis 37:8-9). Imagine how terrible life could be for Joseph in the house where his ten elder brothers hated him. How do you think he could cope with the hatred of his ten brothers? The house will definitely be too hot for him – there'll be nothing he does that would be right. That was the situation Joseph lived in from his childhood to teenage age.

Pit: When an opportune day came for his brothers, they thought of getting rid of him from the house. Hence, they plotted together and threw him into a dry pit (see Genesis 37: 12-14). Could you imagine what depth of trauma Joseph would have, seeing his brothers conspired against him and cast him into a pit? It was really a deep moment of emotional breakdown for him. Agony of betrayal would cease his soul at that particular moment. It's a moment of extreme mental, emotional and physical pain, seeing one's own brothers practically doing such.

Having cast Joseph into the pit, his brothers sat down to eat. They sat down to celebrate their wicked act (see Genesis 37: 25a). They now have rest of mind and joy, since they had gotten rid of their supposed enemy. Their prime expectation was that Joseph would die and rot in the pit – no one will be able to rescue him. This is wickedness in its highest class. They had already devised a plan to deceive their father that a wild animal killed him.

Slavery: In the meantime, his brothers saw some Ishmaelite traders traveling down the jungle road, heading for Egypt. The sight of the trader made his brothers had a rethink of their plot; they finally pulled him out of the pit and sold him to the traders as slave (see Genesis 37: 28-30). They later killed a goat kid and deep his cloth of many colour in its blood to prove to their father that he was slain by a wild animal.

He was Lied Against and Sent to Prison: While in Egypt, Joseph was greatly favoured. God made him to obtain favour in the sight of Potiphar, his Egyptian master. As a result, he became prosperous in slavery. God's presence with Joseph made prosperity to rest on whatever he laid his hand on. Hence, his master handed him all he had except his wife—Mrs. Potiphar.

That was how Joseph became Chief-slave, having other slaves under his control. During this period, his master's wife lusted after him, because of his physical features; he was such a handsome young man. She seduced and attempted to lure him into sleeping with her but he refused. To get back at poor Joseph, she framed him up and told her husband that he had sexually assaulted her. Hearing this, his master threw him into prison. He was imprisoned unjustly for a long period of time, having no one to plead his cause.

Howbeit, in all the thirteen years of traumatic adversity, Joseph never stopped fearing God; that's the testimony! He never allowed the thirteen years of continuous adversity to make him doubt the providential care of God. The Bible didn't tell us that Joseph queried God for once because of his terrible experiences.

Instead of doubting God, Joseph kept on reposing his trust in Him. And for this, he became an epitome of sound trust in God in spite of adversity. Likewise, his decision to forgive his brothers afterward displayed a height at which God expects contemporary Christians to forgive whoever offends us.

Dear reader, what has been your experience in the pilgrimage? Is your life experience just like that of Joseph? Are you in a long season of adversity, challenges and enigmatic experience? Is your trying time prolonging into several unimaginable years?

Has your intimate friends or even siblings abandoned you because of a prolonged predicament? Or has your parents and wife resigned you to fate, concluding that your seemingly ill-luck can never be turned overnight to good-luck? Are you also already giving up, consenting to the numerous negative comments of people around you? I have good news for you. There's help for you from the Lord.

Your dry fig tree can turn wet and blossom. The barren vineyard of your life can be turned fruitful. The bad news you heard from your medical doctor can be turned to good news. Your hopeless situation can turn hopeful, if you can learn to repose your trust in God. This doesn't have anything doing with whether you're a regular attendee of a church or not. You can be churchy without being godly. You can be a churchy man without reposing your trust in God. The Lord who rewrote Joseph's story can also rewrite yours if you'll do what Joseph did.

Just on a fateful day, God put a permanent termination to the thirteen years adversity of Joseph. He was a prisoner in the morning, but became a prime minister at noon. Our God is a miracle worker. He does whatever He wills at His own time. He's unquestionable.

Your life challenges, no matter how long or terrible, is the raw material He needed to produce a miracle. What you just have to do is to repose your trust continually in Him. When you remove your trust from whatever and whomever you had put it earlier, and sincerely fix it in God, He'll rise for your help.

Friend, you can flourish in drought. The drought-like situation that surrounds you will never affect your fruitfulness and productivity if you can put your trust in God. God had never disappointed a man. He'll surely rewrite your story by performing the miracle of flourishing in drought in your life, home and in your entire endeavor if you can put your complete trust in Him.

Joseph did and it pays him off. He was made a prime minister in the land of his slavery. He reigned over those who were his masters previously. That's what only God can do. May your life become the next contemporary proof of this truth, in Christ's name. Amen.

BLOSSOMING INSIDE STORM

*Seeing the Invisible God
inside Storm Brings Peace
inside Storm!*

Chapter 6
BLOSSOMING INSIDE STORM
The story of the book of Daniel opened with chaos, trouble and war. The king of Babylon, Nebuchadnezzar, came to Jerusalem and besieged it. And God deliberately gave him victory over His people. He killed some and carried others, including Jehoiakim their king, away captive to his land.

No one bargains for or wishes to be victim of war because of the horrible, devastating impact it usually has on people's life. As fate would have it, Daniel was among the captives taken to Babylon. By that time, he was young, agile and wise. To be a young man in captivity means excessive labour; the captor would desire you to burn out your strength for him.

Hence, being in captivity was never a funny experience for Daniel and other young Jews in Babylon; it was utter bitterness. He found himself in a storm he never bargained for. But in spite of this storm, Daniel continued to repose his trust in God. He didn't permit the captor to capture his faith though he captured him. He kept on believing and trusting the God of his fathers.

While in the midst of this, an opportunity opened to him and to some other young Jews. It was a royal opportunity. The king needed the service of a number of young men in his royal service, and there was a special demand for Hebrew young men (see Daniel 1:3-4). By divine arrangement, Daniel and his three other friends were part of those selected. They were to be trained in the royal Babylonian University. The areas to cover in their studies include the language of the Chaldeans and literature.

When they started the training, a circumstance required that Daniel and his friends prove the reality of their trust in God. The king had appointed a daily meal and drink from his royal delicacies for everyone selected for the training. Since Babylon was a Gentile kingdom, every food and wine that is prepared in the palace is firstly offered to idols before given to men. Taking from such delicacies means defilement to Daniel and his friends.

Instead of yielding to the royal instruction by taking the meal and wine, they decided to stick out their neck, standing for God.

Read the testimony of the stand of Daniel:

> ***But Daniel purposed in his heart that he would not defile himself with the portion of the king's delicacies, nor with the wine which he drank; therefore he requested of the chief of the eunuchs that he might not defile himself.*** Daniel 1:8

When Daniel took his stand in this respect, three of his contemporaries joined him. Having proved their trust in God through their decision, God Himself rose up to identify with and vindicate them. God gave the four young men knowledge and skill in all literature and wisdom.

Daniel had understanding in all visions and dreams (see Daniel 1:17). God deliberately invested the above mentioned divine treasure into their lives. By implication, they became excellent in their studies. They excelled academically than their counterparts. As a result, they became noticed in the college and were highly respected.

This is a great lesson for some students at all levels who usually think that believing and trusting in God will make them academically poor. God is not a dullard; hence His children are not expected to be poor in whatever they do. He's not a wicked Father, He'll not impoverish His children.

The thought He has for His children are good and wonderful (see Jeremiah 29:11). When you surrender your life to Jesus, He'll forgive you of your sins, cleanse you with His ever pure blood, sanctify you by His word and beautify your life with wonderful heavenly treasures. Christ will take you up, He wouldn't pull you down. You're meant for the top.

Daniel and his friends began to shine and blossom inside the storm. The situations that surrounded them should have pulled them down, but their unflinching trust in God made the difference. They blossomed instead of being dry. It didn't stop there, when the time came for the king to examine them, among them all, none was found like Daniel and his friends. Consequently, they served before the king (see Daniel 1:19).

In all matters of wisdom and understanding about which the king examined them, he found Daniel and his friends ten times better than all the magicians and astrologers who were in all his realm (see Daniel 1:20). Their trust in God made them greatly distinct. There was none like them in the whole kingdom. They were ten times better than the wise men and the philosophers of their time. Their excellence became so noticed that the king always wanted to see them; so he created space for them in the palace. Best men are meant for best opportunities!

That, still, was not the peak for Daniel, he continued to excel till he served with about three different kings. He interpreted enigmatic dreams and read an angel's handwriting on the wall. Daniel's trust in God really pedestalled him on the platform of gold. He was highly spiritual, academically sound, administratively excellent and professionally unmatched.

He set a record in the world of spirituality, academics, administration, politics, etc. that are difficult to comprehend. Can you imagine what earned him this great estate of achievement? His unwavering trust in God. May God help you to put your trust in Him.

GLOWING IN THE FIRE

Are You Afraid of Fire? It's the Right Element that keeps you Shining!

Chapter 7
GLOWING IN THE FIRE

One of the spectacular stories in the Bible is that of Daniel chapter three. The passage bears the account of the encounter and manifestation of Hananiah, Mishael and Azariah who were given the Babylonian names: Shadrach, Meshach and Abednego. We discussed them in the previous chapter.

They were three young men who were contemporaries and close friends of Daniel. They and Daniel were excellent in academics when they were selected for royal training. They were found ten times better than their counterparts, the wise men and the philosophers in the entire kingdom of Babylon. You would recall we said that in the previous chapter.

However, a day came that the King, Nebuchadnezzar, set up a golden image and decreed that everyone in his kingdom must worship it. The fact that Shadrach, Meshach and Abednego were in king's service made it mandatory for them to obey the king's ordinance. The king's decree really set a platform for the three Hebrew men to prove the sincerity of their trust in God. They were brought to the state of decision.

It is either they obey God or Nebuchadnezzar. Meanwhile God had instructed His people, the Jews, not to bow in worship to any other God apart from Him (see Exodus 20:3-5). Obeying king Nebuchadnezzar is disobeying the King of kings. Now they have to take a side, whether God's or Nebuchadnezzar's. Deciding to stand with God will definitely put their lives on line; the king had prepared a burning fiery furnace for whoever dare to contravene his decree. He had decreed that whoever disobeys his order will be roasted alive.

Alas, the three brothers courageously decided for God and were willing to stick out their necks; they dare King Nebuchadnezzar; they flout his order, not minding the repercussion. They decided to party with God. They saw the king's decree as precious opportunity for them to prove their trust in God. On the dedication day of the image, these three Hebrews took their stand – they refused to bow in worship to the molten image. They remain standing while others bowed till they were noticed by natives who reported them to the king. Here is the content of their report:

> ***There are certain Jews whom you have set over the affairs of the province of Babylon: Shadrach, Meshach, and Abed-Nego; these men, O king, have not paid due regard to you. They do not serve your gods or worship the gold image which you have set up.*** Daniel 3:12

Hearing this report, King Nebuchadnezzarcommand the three Hebrews to be brought before him and immediately the three of them were led to the king's presence. Then the king asked them if what he heard was true; they confirmed it! However, they were set of young men he cherished and admired so much so he gave them opportunity to have a rethink and change their stand, at least pretend in the presence of the people. Otherwise ***…you shall be cast immediately into the midst of a burning fiery furnace. And who is the god who will deliver you from my hands?***Said the king. (See Daniel 3:15b)

The three Hebrew brothers refused to compromise and that's how they found themselves in the midst of the king's wrath. The king was enraged to see the brothers flout his order. To worsen it, they weren't natives – they were just mere favoured slaves. Hence, he was ready to make them scapegoat. To him, sparing these will make him appear weak before his people. The king is expected to be firm, strong and sovereign. So to prove himself as the sovereign king, he must roast the three Hebrews in the furnace fire alive.

In the midst of that the three Hebrew friends wouldn't change their stand. They were so zealous for God as to dare the king's wrath. They can't waver in their bold trust in God. They were much confident in the delivering might of God, and spoke of it to the king, not minding his anger. To crown it all, they were even ready to die while standing for God than to be living as cowards and betrayals. They couldn't stand the sight of losing their faith in God to mere threat of death. See their daring response:

O Nebuchadnezzar, we have no need to answer you in this matter.

If that is the case, our God whom we serve is able to deliver us from the burning fiery furnace, and He will deliver us from your hand, O king.

But if not, let it be known to you, O king, that we do not serve your gods, nor will we worship the gold image which you have set up. Daniel 3:16-18

Oh Lord I pray that you'll raise this type of men in your body at this end time in Jesus name. Men who regularly repose their trust in God and will speak for Him before the gentiles courageously, not minding what may be their reaction. Men who had decided to die consecrated, and not defiled. Men who will be so bold to speak of God's power, grace and sovereignty before the unbelievers whether at home or abroad. May God raise you, dear reader, as such men.

The fact is, the scarcity of such men, made the miraculous hand of God rare in our time. We will see God again in His mighty power when the Church stands up to repose her trust in her God. When each believer, not minding whether they are called into full time ministry or not, rise up to stand for their Savior, when each of us stand to represent Jesus in our individual professions, He would definitely demonstrate His power again in the world. The whole world is yet to see what God can do through a man that fear, love and trust Him.

When Nebuchadnezzar heard the response of the men, he was much more tensed in fury. He then commanded that they heat the furnace seven times more than it was usually heated. He then asked choice mighty men in his army to bind Shadrach, Meshach and Abednego, and cast them into the burning fiery furnace. Because the king's instruction was urgent and the furnace was exceedingly hot, the flame of the fire killed the men who threw them into the furnace.

But instead of being burned, unusual miracle happened. God joined them in the fire; hence, the fire couldn't burn these God's generals. They walked and praised God in the fire. They shined and glowed in the fire instead of being consumed by it. Seeing this miraculous sight, the king was astonished; he went close to the entrance of the furnace then asked the brothers to come out.

Afterward, he decreed that every man in his kingdom, whether old or young, male or female etc. must reverence the God of Shadrach, Meshach and Abednego. He added that whoever does otherwise will be cut in pieces. That was how the whole Babylonian empire was captured for God. God became so known throughout the then world, just because three young Hebrews decided to repose their trust in Him (See Daniel 3:28-30).

Dear reader, may your life occasion why God will reveal the mightiness of His power, grace and authority in your time. May the Lord deliver your soul from the fear of death. The fear of death had crippled some children of God from being instrument of honor in God's hand.

The three Hebrews didn't fear death. They saw death stared them in the face yet would not compromise their stand. They didn't because of death remove their trust in God to result to common sense. They didn't stop being spiritual to become rational. Oh Lord, help our generation!

Re-crop our generation! Deliver us from fear. Rescue us from the fear of what to eat, what to wear, where to dwell and where to work. Deliver us from the fear of professional and political threat. Break the gene of fear of persecution, opposition, hatred and death. Make us a set of spiritually, mentally and emotionally bold men, who can rise up to defend what we believe (The Truth about Jesus Christ). Help us to be true to the faith of our fathers. May the banner of faith not go down on us.

PROSPERITY DURING FAMINE

When God wants to Perform Miracle in your Life He puts you in a Situation that Defies Human Assistance!

Chapter 8
PROSPERITY DURING FAMINE
The famine time is a period of unproductivity and stagnancy. Everywhere will be dry; there will not be sowing and reaping because there won't be seed to sow; famine compels people to consume their seeds. Since there is no more food in the ban people are bound to eat whatever they can find edible.

Call to mind the famine in the days of Elisha. Ben-Hadad, the king of Syria gathered all his army, and went up to besiege Samaria. Because of this, famine broke forth in the whole of the city of Samaria. The famine became so great that a donkey's head was sold for eighty shekels of silver and one kab of dove droppings for five shekels of silver.

The famine later moved to an advanced stage that some women started to kill and boil their children as meal just to survive. The king could no longer sit conveniently in the palace; his palace was not exempted (see 2 Kings 6:24-30). The time of famine is a pathetic period.

It's a period of chaos, scarcity and barrenness. Besides, it's also a time of death for many people, especially; the weak ones who couldn't endure prolong stress and lack of food. May you, your loved ones and I never experience famine in Jesus'name.

Just as no one usually wished that evil should happen, by fate, a famine broke out in the days of Isaac. The famine was so severe that Isaac was contemplating going to Egypt for survival. He was ready to leave the Promised Land for Egypt in order to survive the famine.

This reveals how severe the famine was. It was so severe that the covenant child was ready to sacrifice the covenanted land for survival. Nobody can engage in sowing because attempting to do so will result in a waste of seed. The climatic, atmospheric and edaphic condition of the land was negative (See Genesis 26:1).

In the above described time, God came to Isaac and instructed him not to go to Egypt; rather he should dwell in Gerar. Then, He promised to bless him and fulfill the oath He sworn to Abraham his father. (See 26:2-3). He also told him:

> *And I will make your descendants multiply as the stars of heaven; I will give to your descendants all these lands; and in your seed all the nations of the earth shall be blessed;*
>
> *because Abraham obeyed My voice and kept My charge, My commandments, My statutes, and My laws.* Genesis 26:4-5

Hearing these, Isaac obeyed God, defying the reality of the famine which stared him in the face. He judged God faithful and dwelled in Gerar (See 26:6). Then He sowed in that land, and reaped in the same year a hundred-fold of his seeds – God greatly blessed him as He promised (See 26:12). Below are the rest of the testimonies of his prosperity in famine period:

> *The man began to prosper, and continued prospering until he became very prosperous;*
>
> *for he had possessions of flocks and possessions of herds and a great number of servants. So the Philistines envied him.* Genesis 26:13-14

Isaac became so prosperous in famine that he became a threat for the Gerar natives. Hence, they envied him. He so much prospered in his farming business to the extent that the attention of the whole city was drawn to him. His prosperity became the talk of the city. God's identity and blessing on his business set agenda of discuss for the citizens of the land.

I wish you really understand what God did for Isaac. Imagine the implication of when a man's wealth is greater than the wealth of the whole city. That implies he had great influence on the economy of the city. If he should stop supplying his product, the city economy may collapse. That was how great God made Isaac to become just because of his trust in Him.

What Helped Isaac?

He had ability to hear from God

This presupposes that Isaac must have developed a cordial personal relationship with God. His father, Abraham must have taught him what having personal relationship with God means, its importance and how to develop one. Isaac could have had difficulty in hearing and identifying God's voice if he had not been communing and conversing with Him.

Likewise, it would have also been difficult for God to communicate him if he is not a friend. This is a serious foundational lesson for whoever wants to experience life-long flourishing. You need a personal relationship with God. Having this will make it possible for Him to communicate with you.

It will be practically impossible for him to give you needed information, ideas or instruction that'll lead you into spiritual and physical prosperity if you don't develop and maintain a continuous personal relationship with Him.

Men who lack personal relationship with God will be stranded in the year of drought. Elimelech made his family to have this traumatic experience. His lack of personal relationship with God made him to lead his family to Moab when there was famine in Bethlehem where they were living.

He consequently lost his life and that of his two sons, turning his wife to a widow suddenly as well as his daughters-in-law (See Ruth1:1-5). May you not be stranded in the year of drought. You need to develop a personal relationship with God; if that won't happen.

Obedience

Having heard God, he obeyed Him. He didn't attempt to edit God's instruction with his common sense. He knew and accepted that God is wiser than himself, and that His foolishness is wiser than men. His step of obedience proved his belief in God. He didn't doubt or play joker with Him.

This is also an important lesson for whoever desires to flourish in drought. You have to believe practically in God. You have to believe in Him before you can obey Him.

He took a practical step of faith

Isaac did not just remain inGerar doing nothing; he sowed seeds, not minding the prevalent famine. He wasn't like some contemporary Christians who receive many of God's promises only to remain idle without taking practical step of faith. The promises of God to such remain dormant.

Every promise of God usually comes with human responsibility. You are expected to activate the fulfillment of God's promise by carrying out the responsibility the promise required. Take for instance, God promised to bless Isaac greatly during famine.

Isaac understood that God is not a magician; hence, He wouldn't physically rain down the blessing directly from heaven. If He will bless him, he will bless him through the work of his hands. That was why he had to plough the ground and sow his seed. His blessing and liberation is not in staying idle. God's blessing can't rest on an idle man, no matter the number of divine promises he had received.

Irresponsibility is a major thing making the body of Christ to be poor and weak today. We are poor not because God hadn't promised us; we're poor because we fail to take responsibility the fulfillment requires. God Himself is not lazy; He can't bless a lazy man; be responsible! Dear reader, if God had promised to give you a land in a particular region, why don't you relocate there – start sowing there? It will prove if indeed your faith is rather hanging in God.

He was a child of covenant

Isaac was not an ordinary child; he was a covenant child. A divine covenant hung on his head as he grew up. He was born to fulfill a destiny. Some ignorant fellow might want to excuse themselves here. But the fact is, there is no one on earth that is born without a purpose to accomplish.

Every child of God is a destined individual. This truth was disclosed to Jeremiah at the early part of his walk with God. He was practically told by God that, ***"Before I formed you in the womb I knew you, before you were born I sanctify you; I ordained you a prophet to the nations."*** (Jeremiah 1:5)

Hence, children of God are covenanted and destined set of people. God's thought toward us is that of good and not of evil to give us an expected end (See Jeremiah 29:11). Sequel to this, there should be no one who should think his life is inferior to that of Isaac.

He was covenanted, you are also covenanted. Your prosperity should know no season, spiritually and physically. You are to flourish in the year of drought. You are destined for greatness. But you should learn to repose your trust continually in God. That's the master key to continuous flourishing.

FLOURISHING DESPITE OPPOSITION

Your Critics will eventually make you if you know How to handle them!

Chapter 9
FLOURISHING DESPITE OPPOSITION
The story of Nehemiah is famous in the Old Testament portion of the Bible. He had been carried captive to a strange land. Without doubt, Nehemiah was favoured to have been appointed as the king's cup bearer in his land of captivity. While all other captives – his kinsmen – were put to hard labour in the field of their captors, Nehemiah would stand before the king to serve him wine. That was really a rear privilege.

In the meantime, some of his people came from Jerusalem and he inquired from them the state of Jerusalem city. This was the reply they gave him: *"The survivors who are left from the captivity in the province are there in great distress and reproach. The wall of Jerusalem is also broken down, and its gates are burned with fire."*(Nehemiah 1:3). This type of information is saddening and heart shattering.

But really it is awesome to know that despite Nehemiah's captivity, he still had passion for the survivors. He had mind to know their state. Anyway he had been so passionate about his homeland – Jerusalem. Having heard the perplexing report, he contacted a burden for the rebuilding of the walls; the city of his fatherland rehabilitated and its gates re-fixed. See what Nehemiah did when he heard the report:

> *…I sat down and wept, and mourned for many days; I was fasting and praying before the God of heaven.*
> Nehemiah 1:4

Consequent to his sincere prayer to God, Nehemiah obtained favour from the king and was released with provisions to rebuild the broken walls. But when he came to Jerusalem for the rebuilding, he was faced with diverse oppositions. Some people teamed up and made themselves Hebrews' enemies. Sanballat, Tobiah, Geshem the Arab were their names. Of course, their enemies were more than three, but the above three were ring leaders.

The Oppositions within which Nehemiah Flourished

Opposition by Ridicule

As soon as the enemies discovered that the remnant of Israel gathered to rebuild the broken walls of their city, they became indignant. Hence, they promptly gather to ridicule what they were doing. Below are their ridiculous words:

What are these feeble Jews doing? Will they fortify themselves? Will they offer sacrifices? Will they complete it in a day? Will they revive the stones from the heaps of rubbish — stones that are burned?

...whatever they build, if even a fox goes up on it, he will break down their stone wall. Nehemiah 4:2-3

Those words were highly ridiculous; especially when it came at the beginning of the assignment – when the Israelites were just gathering momentum and courage for the project. It's like watering down their decision, courage and zeal to rebuild the wall. The fact is, their enemies were happy about their deplorable state.

Their defenselessness was their highest satisfaction. They actually don't want them to gather up as a people again. They want the Jews to bear their shame, distress, ridicule and to maintain their scattered state forever. They wanted them to be slaves forever – trampled under the feet of their captors.

Friend, this is also the focus and agenda of the devil about you. He's happy about your deplorable state – he is happy you are ravaged and defeated by sin. Seeing your life scattered and broken down by sin gives him the highest joy. He wants you to remain forever vulnerable to self, sin and the forces of the world. That's why he usually discourages you from taking any step that leads to deliverance.

He discourages you from attending fellowship, church services, and genuine conferences… from where you can be offered needed help. He made you to terribly hate the Bible. Sometimes, when you struggle to read, the stories in the Bible don't make meaning to you. Due to this, you just abandon reading the Bible that bears the truth that can set you free.

But let's see how Nehemiah handled the ridiculous oppositions. Instead of returning derogatory words to the enemies, Nehemiah prayed to God who commissioned him for the assignment. Below are his prayers:

> ***Hear, O our God, for we are despised; turn their reproach on their own heads, and give them as plunder to a land of captivity!***
>
> ***Do not cover their iniquity, and do not let their sin be blotted out from before You; for they have provoked You to anger before the builders.***
> Nehemiah 4:4-6

Nehemiah didn't engage in bartering words with the enemy. Not even a word dropped from his lips rather, he consciously talked to God about them. He handed them over to God—he never planned a revenge mission, attack or counter-opposition; not at all! He knew what the enemy (devil)was up to; he knew already that it was a scheme tilted towards distracting him to delay the work. Tell you what, should he had reacted the work wouldn't have finish when they completed it.

A number of commissioned children of God are grounded; theycould not finish their divine assignment because they gave in to responding in words and in some other means to men who ridiculously opposed the work. You can't be responding to the enemy and be able to do or carry out divine assignment; it doesn't work that way! The two can't go together. Any time given to responding personally to the ridiculous attack of men on the assignment in your hand is a minus from the overall time to carry out the assignment.

Instead of making out time to respond to the enemy, we are to do what Nehemiah did. He prayed to God instead of responding to his enemies. He handed them over to Him by reporting their deeds to Him. And having done that, he set his focus on the work he was doing. Responding personally to the ridiculous words of the enemy might degenerate into a chaos that would either temporarily stop or permanently terminate the building of the wall. May our generation learn from Nehemiah's approach to ridicule.

Opposition by Discouraged Brethren

At a point in time when the work was on, some brethren in Judah became discouraged and said to Nehemiah: *"The strength of the laborers is failing, and there is so much rubbish that we are not able to build the wall. And our adversaries said, they will neither know nor see anything, till we come into their midst and kill them and cause the work to cease."* (Nehemiah 4:10-11) This was another challenging opposition Nehemiah had to get solution to; so the work may not stop.

What did he do? How did he handle it? Instead of being fearful, Nehemiah boldly and strategically positioned some men to be at watch against the enemy with weapons of war in their hands. Likewise, he equipped those who labored in the construction with artilleries to defend themselves provided there is an invasion of the enemy.

They held construction equipment in one hand and sword on the other. When their enemies discovered that their secret planshave been discovered, they rescinded. Hence, the building of the wall continued (see Nehemiah 4: 13-23).

Opposition by Craftiness

Having failed in their plan of secret attack, the enemy of the Jew then planned crafty solemn meeting with Nehemiah and accompanied his invitation with a threat letter. The purpose of this is that the work may cease; the project had reached to hanging pillars, gates and doors. Nehemiah didn't stop the work, he only sent messengers back to the enemy that he doesn't have time for such meeting.

He plainly told them that the work he is doing was so great than to stop it for their planned meeting. He doesn't have time for talk when he ought to act (see Nehemiah 6:1-9). After all, the allegations leveled against him and the Jews were unrealistic.

Contemporary Christians need to learn here. It's not every meeting that you must attend. When the enemy allege you of unrealistic offence and ask you to come for dialogue, don't attend such a meeting. Such meeting is arranged to discourage you, harm or take your life, if possible. Sequel to this, men of destiny got to be careful and sensitive to the leading of the Spirit. Besides, they are also expected to be men of balanced IQ – they should be able to reason well, by this they would detect the traps of the enemy.

Within all the above listed oppositions, Nehemiah flourished. The wall of Jerusalem was completely built, its doors and gates were fixed. Having accomplished the task, he returned to Shushan as he promised the king. Dear friend, you can also flourish in opposition, just like Nehemiah did; if you'll completely repose your trust in God and be determined to make impact.

If you're determined to fulfill your God-given vision despite obvious opposition; God will help you. God is ready to help you as He did to Nehemiah. Remove your trust from whatever and whoever you've earlier put it and wholly repose it in God. Life and destiny opposition will not sink you in Jesus' name. Amen.

THE RECURRING DECIMAL

Emphasis Strengthens Memory

Chapter 10

THE RECURRING DECIMAL

Casting a careful look on the flourishing stories of people told in the last six chapters of this book, it's clear that there are recurring decimals common to all the stories. Some factors kept on appearing in the way those people flourished in their particular seasons or situations of drought. The principles taught in chapters three and four of this book are common factors in their stories. Friend, can you remember those principles right now?

Well, let me help you out. They are: *Reposing Your Trust Continually in God; Living a Righteous Life; Being Planted in God's Presence; Having Positive Thoughts; Speaking Positively; Acting Positively; Receiving Specific Direction from God; and Sowing in the Difficult Times.* For clarity, I'll make brief highlights on each of the stories. Going through the highlights will reinforce the potency of the principles to you. Let's go straight into it right now.

Esther and Mordecai

These two Hebrews confidently reposed their trust in God continually despite the drought of bereavement and captivity that came their way. This was demonstrated in Mordecai's insistence to keep his godly consecration in the strange land and Esther's decision to observe three days fast and to appear before the king, not minding the consequence. Without doubt, both of them lived righteously – it was basically for this that Haman hated Mordecai and decided to destroy the whole Jew race found in the empire.

Their decision to pray through their challenge proved that they were conscious of God's awesome presence and power. Till they overcame the determined destruction mission of the enemy, Mordecai and Esther thought, spoke and acted positively – they didn't resign to fate. And lastly, they acted as they sensed being led by God – that was why their steps produced eternal result.

Joseph

For about thirteen years period of varied adversities that Joseph had, his trust in God and righteous living were obviously constant. Even when his righteous life landed him unjustly in prison, he waited patiently for God's vindication – he didn't cut corners for himself. Besides, the Bible emphasized that God was with him in all his adversities – this connotes Joseph was a man of divine presence.

His life was rooted in God's presence – hence, he was prosperous (see Genesis 39:2-3). Throughout of his period of continuous catastrophe, Joseph neither thought nor spoke negatively. His dispositions and actions toward God and human beings were purely positive. He also lived by divine leading – that enabled him to interpret the prophetic dreams of his co-prisoners and Pharaoh. The story of Joseph clearly teaches us that some catastrophes are catapults in disguise.

Daniel

Daniel's story is characterized with trust in God from start to finish. He was known for absolute trust in God, righteous living, divine presence, positive thoughts, words and actions, and was a man that never gambled with life and governmental decisions or policies. These were factors that made him to shine in difficult times. He interpreted mysterious dreams and gave meaning to enigmas. He became so popular as a godly government administrator even in the midst of corrupt counterparts.

Righteousness exalts him exceedingly such that he had to serve with about three military regimes in a strange land. Daniel's story teaches Christian politicians and government administrators that you can flourish in your career if you would stand for righteousness in the midst of corruption. The Bible says, you love righteousness and hate iniquity; that's why the Lord your God anointed you with the oil of gladness above your counterparts (see Hebrews 1:9).

The Three Hebrews

Hananiah, Mishael and Azariah flourished in Babylon because of their trust in God and righteous life. They were also men of God's presence – that was why they were able to partner with Daniel in praying to discover the king's mysterious dream. They thought, spoke and acted positively when the king threatened to burn them alive. They didn't gamble with life decision – they convincingly knew that they were born to live for God.

That was why they stood for Him even when standing for God has death consequence. Through these brothers God performed an unmatchable miracle – instead of burning in the fire they glow evidently for people to see. Consequently, God was globally recognized and worshiped. The story of the three Hebrew brothers teaches us that God appears to us in our standing, not in our resolution to stand for Him.

Isaac

To say Isaac didn't repose his trust in God is to deny the authenticity of his story. While not overlooking the fact that he earlier wanted to run to Egypt without consulting God, we need to acknowledge the simplicity of his heart to obey God when he was instructed to stay in Gerar. He had ability to hear from God because of his righteous life.

Right from when God instructed him to stay in the land ravaged with famine, his thought, words and actions became positive about the challenge(s). He believed God was able to bless him despite the prevalent famine. And just like he adjudged God, he was miraculous blessed during the devastating time. He became outrageously blessed to the extent that the whole city of Gerar envied him. That will be your testimony soon in Jesus' name. Amen!

Nehemiah

Everyone conversant with the story of Nehemiah knows that he was a man who knew, walked with and trusted God. He lived righteously despite the challenges of captivity and reproach of the wall of Jerusalem that was destroyed by his captors. The way he prayed and fasted for forgiveness and restoration of his people shows he was a man of God's presence who knew God's mind.

He thought, spoke and acted positively when the enemy ridiculed the wall he was building and wrongly alleged him of conspiracy. The way he handled the assignment of Jerusalem wall proved that he lived by divine leading – he didn't gamble about the decisions he made. God can help you too as He helped Nehemiah and the rest brethren whose story were told in this book if you will dare to do what they did. All your failures and challenges will soon become testimonies of miracle in Jesus' name. Remain blessed!

Epilogue

YOU SHALL TESTIFY

Do you say "My own is not possible, my dreams are shattered– Mylife, home, business, vision … had hit the rock, all hopes are gone – I can neither flourish nor rise again." You can always dream again, my friend. God can bring hope to your hopeless situation. Out of the rubbles of your life, home, business and vision, He can bring out beauty and productivity. Do you know that it is not yet over until it's over?

Christ can still write a new chapter of the book of your life. Only the dead have no hope. As much as you are breathing, there is hope for a living dog than a dead lion. Out of the shattered pieces of your life, God will bring forth an edifice of glory. Don't be discouraged, Christ will turn your story to glory. He will turn your zero to a hero. Your sun will rise and shine at its full strength again across nations. Instead of shame you shall have double honour.

Can you just imagine a potter who makes a clay pot? And for one reason or the other a pot is marred in his hand. Do you know this potter can break down the pot totally? And out of the broken pieces bring forth a vessel that is more beautiful than the former.

Your life might have been disfigured by whatever reason – by a mistake you made or a wrong step you took. Don't give up! What you're going through now is the breaking of the potter. Afterward he's going to bring forth something glorious. Out of the broken pieces of your life God is going to bring forth something useful for His glory. Jesus loves you – He is interested in your case.

Whatever type of drought you currently experience – spiritual, academic, professional, social, marital, ministerial, financial, material, emotional, psychological or economical – that experience will turn to raw material for God to produce a miracle. This will happen if you can repose your total trust in God, love righteousness and live righteously, and become a resident of God's presence.

This exactly is the truth this book teaches. Once you give Him space, God will have mercy on you. He will give you beauty for ashes, the oil of joy for mourning and the garment of praise for the spirit of heaviness. He will lift you up out of the miry clay; He will set your feet upon the rock. He will give you a new song – He will wipe away your tears. No more shall you be desolate, you shall be called Beulah and Hephzibah.

O you afflicted one, tossed with tempest, and not comforted, behold, I will lay your stones with colorful gems, and lay your foundations with sapphires. I will make your pinnacles of rubies, your gates of crystal, and all your walls of precious stones. All your children shall be taught by the Lord, and great shall be the peace of your children. In righteousness you shall be established; you shall be far from oppression, for you shall not fear; and from terror, for it shall not come near you. Indeed, they shall surely assemble, but not because of Me. Whoever assembles against you shall fall for your sake, says the Lord.(Isaiah 54:11-15)

You are next to share testimony!

**Do you have any question or clarification?
Did you make a decision while reading this book?
You will need help in following it through!
Write, Call or contact:
+2347030198431, +2348061693479,
+2348032185648
+2348065976397, +2347031600360,
+2347039298883
<u>livingspringpublication@gmail.com</u>,
<u>vogsnetwork@gmail.com</u>,
And do it now before the devil changes your mind!!!**

Appendix
Winning With Jesus in Prayer

Beloved, join us to pray for the unsaved souls in your locality, state, nation and in every nations of the world on Thursdays of every week. Prayer starts by 12 noon – 12midnight, which may include fasting if you are privileged. How to go about it;

1. Choose an hour (1 hour) out of the 12 hours.

2. Choose a convenient place (venue) for yourself (the place should be good for communion with God; free from distraction).

3. Use the hour you have chosen to intercede for the unsaved souls, light of the gospel of Christ in dark nations of the world, missionaries on the fields and their families, pastors, teachers of the word, evangelists etc. Also ask God to release a fresh genuine passion for the lost souls into your heart. Thank God for hearing your request.

4. Pick a specific unsaved soul, village, town or city to pray for as God leads you.

> *Therefore I exhort first of all that supplications, prayers, intercessions, and giving of thanks be made for all men, for kings and all who are in authority, that we may lead a quiet and peaceable life in all godliness and reverence. For this is good and acceptable in the sight of God our Savior, who desires all men to be saved and to come to the knowledge of the truth.* (1Timothy 2:1-4 NKJV)

This is a solemn call to every genuine sons and daughters of God in all places, *"He who gathers in summer is a wise son; He who sleeps in harvest is a son who cause shame." "And he who wins souls is wise."* (Proverbs 10:5; 11:30b NKJV). May the Lord grant you understanding and grace to tarry on your knees in Jesus name. Amen.

If you have decided to start this prayer, text "YES I WILL" with your name and personal phone number on any of these phone lines: +2347030198431 or +2348032185648. We will be sending text messages to you to keep reminding you your decision.

Also, if you have anyone around you who have not given his or her life to Jesus and you believe God for the change of the person's life, send the person's full name, phone number, e-mail address and the description of the person's current state of life on sola4christmission@gmail.com or david4mission@gmail.com . You could also forward it to +2347030198431 or +2348065976397. We are ready to present the life of the person to God in prayer and to also reach out to him or her.

All enquires about this book to:

Living Spring Publications Network
Living spring Communications
P.O. Box 1961, Ogbomoso, Oyo State, Nigeria
Tel: +2347030198431, +2348115213552
livingspringpublication@gmail.com

You can obtain copies of this book from the following places/contacts:
Living Spring Communications
Poly Mini Mart, The Federal Polytechnic, Ede, Osun State
+2347030198431, +2348032185648

Living Spring Communications
Owo, Ondo State
+2347031600360

C/o Rev. David Olawuyi
Chaplain, Lautech Interdenominational Chapel, Ogbomoso
+2348065976397
C/o RemiAdejumo
Zion Baptist Church, 221, Yoruba Road, Minna
+2348038569014

We want to hear from you. Please send your comment about this book to us in
care of: livingspringpublication@gmail.com

Or write to the address below:

Living Spring Publications Network
Living Spring Communications
P.O. Box 1961 Ogbomoso, Oyo State, Nigeria

Thanks

About the Book

A preacher said, adversity is a university of necessity for prosperity to thrive. When God is all you believe solution is all that you receive. The worst kind of drought is to be in drought but count it as normal situation. Man in the journey of life had been at various junctures of confusion and such needs help for direction which can only be instructed by the Divine.

Therefore, the writer has been helped both by God and of God to discover that man needs to flourish in spite of any predicament of life, solution from God should distinct the follower and believer of God. As Sun is not deterred by nature in its time to shine, so the glory of God must be evident in the life of ardent seeker and believer of God. If otherwise, God is never at fault but where man puts his trust, hope and faith.

Drought is a universal predicament that manifests in different dimensions and occasions of life. However, its solution is solely and fundamentally applicable, accessible, reachable and available in God through Jesus Christ. Going through this book at this moment will sparer the reader from being a victim of drought especially in this dispensation wherein all that could be termed drought is making suicide action the first option thereby populating hade. The solutions proffered though believed to be inspired in this book has divine instructions beyond secular expertise to make the reader a better informed person and liberated to live for God no matter the difficult situation that may feature in the course of pilgrimage in life.

Get it. Read it. Reach it. Apply it.

Dn Jesse Aremu
CEO, Jesses Professional Consult,
Abuja.

Jesus is the Lord of all seasons and times. He is the Lilly of the valley, the Bright and Morning Star. He changes times and seasons. He's the only one who can sleep during storms of life; He's the only one who can make you flourish in drought. This is because He is the Way, the Truth and the Life. Wherever He faces is the way. This is why He can make you flourish even in drought.

And Isaac sowed in the land and reaped hundred folds, even in drought. Jesus is the solution to economic crises; He's the solution in all seasons including drought.The Lord is going to use this book to calm the storms in your life, home and profession and make you flourish like palm tree, like cedar in Lebanon, for "those who are planted in the house of the Lord shall flourish in the courts of our God… they shall be fresh and flourishing". (Psalms 92:13-14) Flourishing in Drought!!!

Dr Samson Olajide Olaniyan
Economics Department, Osun State University, Okuku.

About the Author

Sola Alabi is called into strategic mission work. He is committed to presenting the messages of the gospel of Christ in permanent form (print form of communication) and the reproduction of the very Life of Jesus in the growing youth. The latter form his regular involvement in High School and Campus Missions. Apart from this publication, he has been privileged to write some numbers of other titles in Living Spring Communications series. These include: "The Living Corpse," "From Church to Hell," "Church: The Only Hope of Christ," "Needed Lessons for Kingdom's Pilgrims," "What do you Seek?" and lots more. Sola studied Mass Communication at The Federal Polytechnic, Bida, Niger State and Theology at Baptist College of Theology, Oyo, Oyo State. He is happily married to Olufunke. He currently serves Christ under the umbrella of Living Spring Network, a body committed to soul winning and discipleship.

www.ingramcontent.com/pod-product-compliance
Lightning Source LLC
Chambersburg PA
CBHW070253230526
45470CB00002B/590